The Wonderful World of

Young Animals

The Wonderful World of

Young Animals

Cathy Kilpatrick

Hamlyn
London · New York · Sydney · Toronto

Published by The Hamlyn Publishing Group
Limited
London · New York · Sydney · Toronto
Astronaut House, Feltham, Middlesex, England

Copyright © The Hamlyn Publishing Group
Limited 1978
ISBN 0 600 39537 5

Phototypeset by Photocomp Limited,
Birmingham, England.
Colour separations by Vidicolour Limited,
Hertfordshire, England.
Printed in Spain by Mateu Cromo, Madrid.

Contents

Introduction

Below
Although blind and naked at birth, baby mice are still recognizable as such and instinctively know how to obtain milk from their mother.

Far right
A baby Gorilla (*Gorilla gorilla*) in the safety of its mother's arms. Most mammals show parental care to their offspring, teaching them how to find food and care for themselves in their surroundings.

Overleaf
Parental care in invertebrates (animals without backbones) is rare. A mother scorpion, however, carries its pale young, which are born alive, on her back.

Throughout the world of nature, whenever we see a young animal we are usually aroused with feelings of tenderness and affection towards it. Most of us love to see a human mother feeding her new baby, or newborn kittens, blind and almost naked, nuzzling up to their mother in order to suckle her milk. In the countryside in spring, it is a delightful sight to see young lambs playing and romping around their field. It is also a wonderful experience to observe quietly from a hiding place, a nest in your garden when the eggs have hatched and the parents are busy flying to and fro with copious amounts of grubs and caterpillars to feed their hungry brood.

Some newborn animals, like the lambs and human babies, differ only slightly in appearance from their parents but are far smaller. Other animals only take on a more adult appearance as they develop. A baby kangaroo, for example, looks like an embryo when born and it is only after weeks of development in its mother's pouch that it takes on the familiar adult kangaroo form. Other babies are completely different at birth from the adult form and only take on the adult shape after one of a succession of moults known as metamorphoses. A beautiful butterfly, for example, hatches from its egg into a hungry caterpillar, which after eating and moulting several times, changes or metamorphoses into a resting, pupal stage, spending weeks as a chrysalis. Within this case amazing chemical and physical changes are performed and at last an adult butterfly emerges with crushed wings, which are unfurled and dried in the sun.

Sometimes a newborn animal is completely independent and cares for itself without ever meeting or seeing its parents. Creatures of the sea such as starfishes, molluscs, sea anemones, crabs and fishes, and amphibians, reptiles and the majority of insects and other lower invertebrates are independent babies. Although they are able to lead their own lives, millions of them perish within minutes, hours or days of birth, because there are so many pressures placed upon them by nature. A large number are eaten,

After pairing, adult Privet Hawk Moths (*Sphinx ligustri*) part and the female lays her eggs on the leaves of privet. A tiny caterpillar hatches from each egg and after a time changes into a pupa or chrysalis. Inside this case amazing chemical and physical changes take place and at last the adult moth, or imago, emerges, its main aim in life being to find a mate and produce offspring.

while others die from cold or the inability to obtain food. However, the numbers of young born to one parent are large enough so that sufficient young survive to ensure the continuation of the species.

The earliest organisms, which evolved on Earth millions of years ago, probably reproduced by simply splitting themselves into two when they had reached a certain size. This asexual method of reproduction known as binary fission (splitting in two) or multiple fission (splitting into many) is found in tiny organisms such as bacteria, and protozoans such as amoeba and euglena.

Fragmentation describes the

breaking up of an animal's body into two or more parts to produce young animals when there are no special sex cells associated with the process. Some aquatic worms do this and the asexual reproductive phase of a jellyfish can be included under this method. Jellyfish produce swimming larvae called planulae which settle on rocks and become fixed. The planula larva grows to look rather like the familiar hydra and is known as a scyphistoma. This feeds and grows during the summer and during winter and spring it splits off tiny young jellyfish or medusae at the free end. These young are called ephyrae and are stacked up like saucers at the end of the body stalk. They break away from the body one by one. Certain sea anemones and corals split into two parts longitudinally to produce young.

Many soft-bodied animals such as hydra and obelia reproduce asexually by *budding*. A small swelling begins to form and grow on the parent and is called a bud. When it is fully formed – a perfect but tiny version of its parent – the bud breaks away from the parent to lead an independent life.

Higher animals in the invertebrate and vertebrate groups reproduce only by sexual means. This reproduction is the result of special sex cells gathered into reproductive organs known as gonads. These produce germ cells or gametes during the life of the sexually mature adult. Each gamete contains, on the chromosomes of its nucleus, a set of genes which are encoded instructions about the make-up of the animal species. Gametes from two individuals of the same species come together and fuse to form a cell known as a zygote. The zygote divides repeatedly, each cell containing two lots of instructions, one from a female and one from a male so that the developing young animal's body will grow eventually into the image of its kind.

Below
A free-swimming larva of the fixed barnacle. This offspring is tiny and looks completely different from its parent, going through various stages until it settles down on a rock and takes on an adult barnacle form.

Bottom
Many soft-bodied animals, such as the Brown Hydra (*Hydra fusca*) illustrated here, reproduce asexually by budding. A small swelling, the bud, grows from the parent's body and develops into a tiny version of its parent before breaking away. Two buds are seen here, one half developed, the other almost ready to lead an independent life.

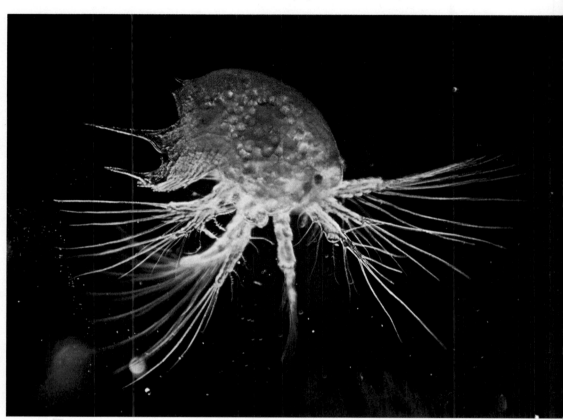

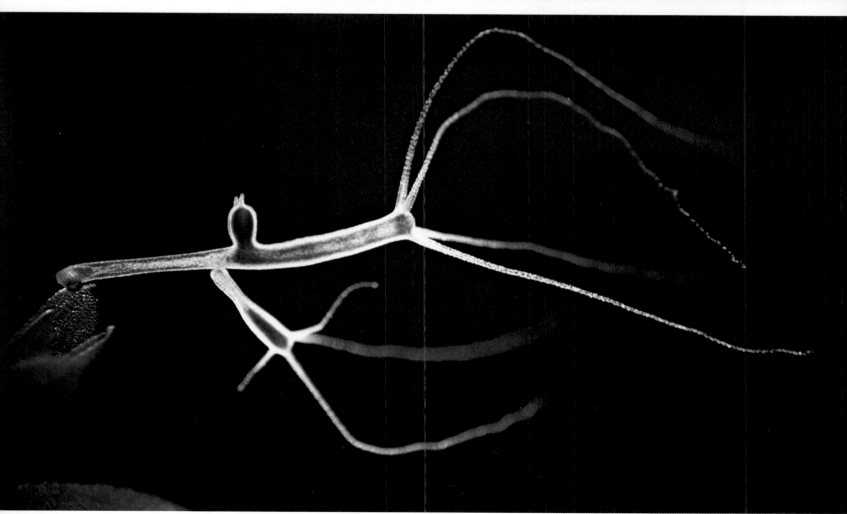

On hatching from their eggs, baby birds are either blind and naked, or have their eyes open and are covered with fine down feathers. Illustrated here is a Flamingo (*Phoenicopterus ruber*) chick covered with down. The special feeding beak seen in the parent will develop as the baby grows.

In most cases of sexual reproduction, there is one female adult producing female sex cells known as eggs or ova which contain a food supply, and male adults producing male sex cells or spermatozoa, which look like microscopic tadpoles with a tiny head and long tail. In many species of lower animals a single adult has both kinds of gametes. Jellyfishes, hydra and earthworms contain both male and

female gametes and these animals are known as bisexual or hermaphrodite. In most higher animals there are two separate sexes, a male and a female, and this phenomenon is known as *sexual dimorphism*. Quite often there are distinct physical characters which distinguish the sexes. In humans, males grow facial hair when maturing, while in monkeys the males often develop colour patches. In deer, the males have horns for fighting other males for females. In many birds it is easy to tell a male from a female. A male Peafowl (*Pavo cristatus*), the Peacock, has wondrous colours, while his mate is rather dowdy, as she needs to be dull coloured to hide herself when sitting on her eggs on a ground nest. However, there are still many species throughout the animal world where it is difficult to tell one sex from another. In the black and white Giant Panda (*Ailuropoda melanoleuca*) it is impossible to tell externally which sex the animal is. In many birds such as the parrots, wrens, owls, penguins and gulls the sexes are similar in outward appearance.

In animals where the sexes are separate, before any baby is born into the mainstream of life, the sexes must get together. Among vertebrate animals, a male and female often engage in ritual displays before accepting one another and bringing their eggs and sperm into contact with each other. In some

Young snakes, like these one-day-old Garter Snakes *(Thamnophis sirtalis sirtalis)*, differ only slightly from their parents but are far smaller.

The Midwife Toad (*Alytes obstetricans*) male winds the eggs, which he has induced the female to lay, round the lower part of his body as soon as he has fertilized them. He carries the eggs in this way for about a month, until they hatch into larvae, and swim away to lead independent lives.

cases, especially among the fishes, the eggs and sperm are simply released into the water. However, there are many variations on the theme of reproduction and not all can be discussed here.

In the higher vertebrates such as most amphibians, reptiles, birds and mammals the sexes form pairs known as pair-bonds. Pair-bonding is a complicated process of behaviour involving selecting mates, courtship displays and rituals, and mating. It can involve selecting sites and building nests and homes for the rearing of the family. In many species, once a pair is formed they stay together for life. This is the case in some mammals such as Lions (*Panthera leo*), apes and monkeys, and many birds such as albatrosses, parrots, eagles, swans and swallows. In others the bond is temporary, lasting for the duration of the breeding season or just until the couple has mated which is the case in most amphibians and reptiles, and many mammals and some birds. During courtship and display the various animal species use many ways of communicating their adoration to the other sex. Some use songs and calls as in birds, frogs, toads and some mammals, such as deer and foxes. Visual signals are also very important, special court-

ship colours developing in many species. The stickleback male, for example, becomes red-bellied and blue-eyed, while the female becomes silvery. In birds, especially where the sexes are different in appearance, the feathers are groomed and grown to the best condition possible for the courtship displays. Consider, for example, the Peacock and his shimmering train, the birds-of-paradise, the lyrebirds and the numerous waterfowl. Although there is great response to each other, there is also usually a strong reaction to other members of their own kind in the form of aggression and hostility. Males will defend their mates and the territory established for the baby animals which will soon be born.

However, whether animals produce their young in a totally impersonal way such as an amoeba simply splitting itself into two, or as a result of a romantic, exciting courtship as in most birds and mammals, the youngsters produced are born to deal with the process of growing up and trying to survive. In the following pages young animals of all shapes and sizes, born in many different places are discussed and beautifully illustrated to reveal many exciting facts about their world.

Domestic baby animals

Most people are familiar with pets such as dogs, cats and gerbils, and farm animals such as cows, sheep, horses, goats and pigs. All these animals are the result of the domestication of these animals' wild ancestors through the centuries by man. A wild animal was probably first caught as a young animal. It seems likely that the dog was the first of these animals to be tamed by man. There are over 165 different breeds of dog in the world today and it is thought that the wolf and the jackal are their ancestors. During the Stone Age, the wild ancestors of the domestic dog no doubt followed the hunters in the hope that they would get the remains of a kill. It seems very likely that their puppies were found and perhaps the hunter's children persuaded their fathers to be allowed to keep the young, attractive puppies. The puppies easily grew to accept their human owner as a substitute parent. We know that even today wild jackal and wolf cubs can be easily tamed and will accept man. The hunters no doubt found out that their canine animal could help them find food with its excellent sense of smell. With the constant presence of wild animals such as bears, wolves, Lions and other hunting animals, coming close to man's settlements, the tamed wild dog was also a useful guard. Later, but still quite early on in the domestication of wild animals, man used dogs to herd and protect his domesticated herds of sheep and goats.

Young puppies today attract the attention and love of most people because of their clear bright eyes, alert expressions, plump bodies and lively, playful manners. Dogs are still used as working animals, guard dogs, hunting dogs and herding dogs, but there is an increasing tendency today to keep them purely and simply as pets, and from all the dog breeds available there is one to suit the prospective, loving owner.

A young puppy is born after about sixty-three days developing inside its mother's womb. The mother licks her puppies clean as they are born and they instinctively find their way to her teats and suckle her milk. The puppies stay under their mother's care and pro-

A bitch lies on her back and lets her puppies feed themselves, although one seems to prefer to sleep!

tection for eight to ten weeks before being parted to go to a new human owner. A puppy at eight weeks is still a baby and, like all babies, needs warmth, lots of love and affection, plenty of rest and small, frequent meals. A puppy should be protected, by an inoculation given by a veterinary surgeon, against hardpad, distemper, canine virus hepatitus and other infections. This is usually given in one injection at around twelve weeks with booster doses when necessary, as advised by your veterinary surgeon.

Nearly every puppy brought away from its mother and brothers and sisters will protest and whimper when it finds itself alone the first night. The first thing you should provide is a good bed. A draught-free box will do, as long as it is lined with old blankets or a soft cushion. It is useful to place a clock under the

puppy's sleeping blanket for the first few nights. The ticking sound will make the young animal less lonely and help train the pet to stay in its bed.

A young puppy is trained by gentleness and firmness. House-breaking is an important part of its education. Feed your puppy at regular intervals and take it outside after each meal. At eight weeks a puppy has a little control over its bladder but will instinctively leave its box before relieving itself. Any soiled spot should be cleaned with strong disinfectant to rid the area of puppy scents. If caught in the act, tap gently on the rump and say clearly 'No! No! No!', then put the puppy out of the house. The amount of food given to a puppy and an adult dog varies according to the breed. Usually your vet, pet-shop owner, or the breeder will give

instructions on the amount suitable for the puppy.

A kitten is a charming and playful member of a household. It is a lively creature and will spend hours amusing itself, but it still needs constant care, love and regular feeding. It is instinctively a clean animal and learns to use a litter tray quite quickly, usually in a few days, unlike a puppy which may take six months.

It is advisable not to take a tiny kitten away from its family until it is ten weeks old unless you can be sure it will get four small meals a day. A kitten does not have to be taken for walks as does a dog, but it can be trained to walk on a lead if desired. A kitten certainly loves a garden to play in, but it will live quite happily in a flat and gets sufficient exercise from chasing a ball or toy around. It loves dozing in a sunny spot either on a window ledge or in a warm spot outside. A kitten grows up very quickly and is adult at around six months of age.

Baby rabbits, gerbils, guinea pigs, hamsters and mice are other animals that are often kept as pets. Rabbits were probably first domesticated in the seventeenth century and kept for food. Later, different varieties were developed and many are now kept as pets. A pregnant doe will begin to make a nest for her babies from her own fur and the cage bedding. The youngsters are born after about thirty days gestation. The blind babies rest and suckle in the nest. At twelve to fourteen days old they open their eyes and have grown fur. They are very pretty to look at and can now be removed from the nest and handled with care. It is most important not to disturb the nest or the mother before this time, or the doe may eat her own babies. The baby rabbit can leave its mother at six weeks when it is eating and drinking by itself. A baby doe will mature at nine months and can have her own youngsters. A buck rabbit is adult at six months.

A baby guinea pig, or cavy to give it its correct name, is best bought when it is six to eight weeks old. At this age it is independent of its mother and is ready to make friends in its new surroundings. A young guinea pig is one of the prettiest babies as it is born fully furred and with its eyes open. Two to seven young are usually born after a gestation period of sixty-three to seventy-five days. After two weeks the babies will be feeding by themselves. They like corn and oats and a little carrot or green food every day. A bran mash meal can be given at night. They also eat dandelion leaves, clover, fruit peelings such as apple and pear, celery and chicory.

Above left
Young domestic animals, although natural enemies when adult in the wild and domestic situation, will soon accept one another if introduced at an early age. These Cocker Spaniel puppies and Chinchilla Persian kitten are amicable playmates.

Above right
Although helpless and blind at birth, a young rabbit has grown its fur and opened its eyes by twelve days, as in the one shown here with its mother affectionately sniffing it.

Right
A favourite pet of many, a Golden Hamster *(Mesocricetus auratus)* mother carefully cleans her blind offspring.

A young foal suckles from its mother. It is already long legged with strong muscles and alert senses, ready to follow its mother or run around its field in play.

They will make their bed out of soft hay which should be changed daily.

Gerbils and jerboas have become very popular as pets as they are charming and amusing. There are more than 100 different species and it is very difficult to identify a particular species. The jerboas have kangaroo-like hind legs that can carry them many feet in a single bound and, consequently, they need quite large cages. All the gerbils are small animals, ranging in size between that of a mouse and a small rat. They are very industrious, seeking out seeds and roots and hiding them in their cage. They will spend hours biting paper or toilet rolls into shreds to make a nest. They are very prolific breeders and sometimes produce as many as fourteen young at a time. The tiny babies are blind and naked at birth. They should not be disturbed or the mother may kill and eat them. After about twenty-one days they will leave the nest and make short exploratory trips. They will soon take their own food and can be separated from their mother.

Young farm animals

To visit a farm in spring or early summer and see the various young mammals is a wonderful experience.

Lambs frolic together, young foals dash about the buttercup-filled meadows, calves look wide-eyed and appealing and kid goats jump on their mother's back playing king-of-the-castle. The average gestation period of a mare is about eleven months (340 days), in the cow nine months (280 days), in the ewe five months (150 days) and in the sow sixteen weeks (112 days). There is, however, variation in all these times depending on the breed.

All domestic horse breeds originate from the Wild Horse (*Equus przewalskii*) which survives in small numbers on the Mongolian Steppes, as well as in captivity. A young foal at birth struggles to its feet within half an hour and totters for a few minutes as it searches for the milk supply. Within a few hours it is dancing around its mother but it is instinctively . wary of anything around it. A young foal's trust has to be won over by a careful approach and gentle stroking and caressing. High-class horse breeding is a science today and much thought goes into choosing a stallion and mare. A good temperament in both parents is essential as well as freedom from hereditary diseases. A thorough-bred foal is usually so valuable that it is born in a special foaling box with a vet and helpers supervising.

Many mares of humbler breeds are quite happy to give birth in their own field, although a watchful eye is usually kept on the mare to make sure she does not get into difficulties. At eight weeks the foal begins to nibble its mother's oats, and at about six to seven months it can be weaned and separated from its mother. The youngster is still in need of a companion, however. Another foal, a good-tempered pony

or a donkey gelding is a good partner. They will become firm friends and nuzzle up at night to keep warm.

Donkeys, mules and asses have been man's beasts of burden for centuries. They are still used to carry people and goods in poorer countries, but in most developed countries donkeys are kept as attractive pets for children.

Sheep, goats and cattle belong to

Life seems already very tiring for this young donkey as it rests against its mother's hind legs.

the same family as buffaloes and antelopes. The domesticated sheep come from wild sheep but it is not known which species is the ancestor. The Mouflon (*Ovis musimon*) probably provided the main breeding stock centuries ago. Sheep are valued commercially for their mutton and wool, and in some countries for their milk.

Before lambing, the ewe flock is usually collected and looked over to check that their teats are clear of wool; otherwise the newborn lambs might swallow wool in their first attempts to suck. Lambing in hill flocks usually takes place in the open, although the shepherd often brings the flock down with the help of his sheepdog to lower pastures in case of bad weather. Lambing generally begins in late spring, although earlier births are not uncommon and these usually find themselves photographed and printed in national papers telling the world that spring is really on the way. The shepherd checks his ewes two or three times a day and helps any ewe in difficulty. Lambs and their mothers are sometimes caught in snowstorms and become buried. The

sheepdog is then most important as it can sniff out buried bodies with its excellent sense of smell.

A ewe generally gives birth to a single lamb, although twins are common and there are usually some triplets. Some lambs are orphaned at birth, their mothers refusing to accept them Sometimes a mother whose lamb has died is happy to accept an orphan lamb. The dead lamb's skin is tied over the back of an orphan lamb and generally the mother accepts it at once. Another device is to rub the ewe's nose with whisky so that she is temporarily deprived of her sense of smell and often does not notice that the new lamb does not smell like her. When these tactics fail, the lamb is usually taken to the farmer's wife who hand-rears the orphan on a baby's feeding bottle. Lambs suckle for about six weeks, although they eat a little solid food within a few days of birth and crop bits of grass at two weeks.

Goats are valued either for their fleeces or their milk. The Cashmere and Angora breeds are the most important goats, reared for their soft, fine wool. The Angora fleece

Domesticated goats in the Koaka Veld, south-west Africa.

provides mohair and in the best specimens it is extremely fine, silky and lustrous. The nanny-goat of this breed usually produces only one kid, twins being rare. Goat's milk is comparable to cow's milk but is richer in fat and poorer in other solids.

Domestic cattle *(Bos taurus)* have been in existence a long time. They are known to have existed in Babylon as early as 5 000 BC. The earliest-known domesticated type found in Europe is a very slightly built ox with short horns, which was very widespread in the Neolithic (polished stone) period. It was probably introduced from Asia where it had long been domesticated. It is sometimes known as the Celtic Shorthorn and was found in Britain until Roman times. In Europe, however, domestic cattle descend from the wild Aurochs *(Bos primigenius)*, enormous long-horned beasts that stood 1·8 metres (6 feet) at the shoulder. The last-known wild specimen was killed in Poland in 1628. A very ancient breed which survives in a few places is the 'wild' white cattle or park cattle. Some zoologists believe the Romans brought them into Europe, while others think they are direct descendants of

Attractive goat kids with their mother. Goat's milk is comparable to cow's milk but is richer in fat and poorer in other solids.

Above
A Scottish Highland calf is an attractive miniature of its parent, except that it has yet to grow its horns and its coat will become longer and shaggier.

Far right
A young calf and mother. A cow is usually mated to give birth to her first calf when three or four years old, and then has a baby each year for the next three or four years.

Overleaf
Twins are quite common in sheep, with triplets being frequent and even quads not a rare happening.

the wild Auroch. Today, the numerous breeds of cattle are kept for their meat, milk and hides, as well as beasts of burden in poorer countries.

A cow is usually mated to produce her first calf when she is two or three years old, and then usually produces a calf a year for three or four years. A calf at birth weighs between 45 and 90 kilograms (100 and 200 pounds) according to the breed and feeding. Most farmers in the Western world organize it so that the mothers reared for milk have their calves in autumn as the milk the mother produces fetches a high price at this time. Those mothers that are producing beef calves are mated so that they have their babies in spring and they feed them through the summer months. However, there is no hard and fast rule.

A young calf soon struggles to its feet and is walking within a few hours. Between two and five hours

after its birth it takes its first milk from its mother's udders searching around its mother's body until it finds a teat. The mother often nudges her offspring in the right direction. If the mother is a milk-producing breed the calf is separated from its mother soon after birth to join other calves which are artificially reared by the farmer, while the mother goes on producing milk for the farmer.

In Africa, Asia and Australia, domesticated cattle breeds with large humps called Zebu *(Bos indicus)* are found which are probably descended from the Malayan Banteng *(Bos banteng)*. These cattle have been bred to resist the infections of the countries and survive on poor quality vegetation and accept the high temperatures.

The pig is a domesticated animal which can produce lots of babies; over twenty being born at a time is

fairly common. Farmers, however, prefer to keep only about twelve with a mother, as although the mother has fourteen teats, the hind pair do not usually give much milk. Surplus piglets, if healthy and vigorous, may easily be transferred to a sow who has given birth to a small litter. She usually accepts foster piglets quite happily. The European pig breeds are descended from the Wild Boar *(Sus scrofa)*. A Wild Boar sow gives birth to five to eight attractive piglets which are brown with stripes running along their bodies. An adult boar is very fierce with razor-sharp tusks with which he can defend himself.

The process of giving birth in pigs is known as farrowing and it may last several hours if the litter is a large one. The sow usually gives birth in special farrowing quarters and, because she is easily excited at this time, it is usual for only her regular farming man to attend her. If she gets upset she may tread or lie on her young, or savage or even eat them. If a sow does kill her young she is not usually bred again. Young piglets are quite sensitive to cold in the first few weeks of their lives and it is necessary for them to have a warm, dry, draught-free pen, which

is often artificially heated. The piglets are weaned at about eight weeks and the mother is removed from their pen.

On a farm you will usually find domestic fowl which originated from Junglefowl *(Gallus gallus)* ancestors that live in south-east Asia. They reached Europe during Christian times and were bred not only for their food value but also for the sport provided by cock-fighting. Today there is a large number of breeds and varieties, each possessing special characteristics. A laying hen produces about 200 eggs or more a year, which is about five or six times her body weight in eggs. Today, with man's demand for chicken's eggs and meat, most hens are not allowed to sit on their eggs as they used to do. Machines have been invented to incubate the chicks, so that the first thing a chick sees on hatching is rows and rows of eggs and one or two other hatching brothers or sisters. Within the first twenty-four hours after hatching, thousands of chicks are on their way to their new owners. A chick grows very fast. At birth it is under 57 grams (2 ounces) and yet it multiplies this weight sixteen times in eight weeks. At this rate, a human

Domestic pigs give birth to twenty or more young piglets, although less than twelve are preferable as this animal has only seven pairs of teats, the last pair not usually giving much milk.

baby of average weight at birth would weigh 50 kilograms (8 stones) at two months old.

Geese, ducks and turkeys are also farmed under these intensive breeding systems on our modern farms. A gaggle of geese and a flock of ducks with their yellow downy chicks are a rare sight in a farmyard today.

There are many other domesticated animals in the world, including elephants, Yak *(Bos grunniens)* Reindeer *(Rangifer tarandus)*, and even camels and their South American relatives the Llamas *(Lama peruana)*. In their native countries they are

very important. In India and Burma the Elephant *(Elephas maximus)* is tamed to carry out work in the timber forests. The baby Elephant is given a name soon after it is born and registered as a C.A.H. – calf at heel. However, for the first five years he is loved, often hand-fed, petted, and has an 'aunt' or two to anticipate his needs. He trails his mother on or off duty, often suckling while she is concentrating on her work, such as dragging a 2-tonne log towards a floating stream. Between the ages of five and sixteen years, the Elephant is weaned,

A farmyard Hen *(Gallus gallus)* and her numerous chicks are a rare sight these days, as millions of chicks hatch in special incubating machines, the eggs being taken from the mother on laying.

trained and taught the various duties of being a working Elephant.

The one-humped Arabian Camel *(Camelus dromedarius)* is no longer found in the wild but domesticated forms range from northern Africa through central to south-west Asia. The two-humped or Bactrian Camel *(Camelus bactrianus)* exists in the wild in the Gobi desert but most alive today are domesticated forms. The first record of a one-humped camel is on pottery dating from the sixth dynasty of Ancient Egypt, about 3 500 BC. Today they are still used in desert and semi-desert areas as they are so well adapted to deal with the harshness of the environment. A baby camel is an identical miniature of its parents except for its front teeth (incisors), its lovely soft fleece, lack of knee pads and

hump. The baby at first only has a soft *baa* but it can walk rather unsteadily on its feet at the end of its first day. The young camel stays with its mother for four years, running at her side on long journeys across the desert. In South America the Llama and Alpaca *(Lama pacos)* have been bred for centuries by the natives. Llamas are mainly used as pack animals, the Alpaca being bred for its fine wool. Llamas also provide wool, meat and hides, and their fat is used for candle-making. As soon as a baby is able to stand (within a few hours of birth), it can run with surprising endurance. The youngster is nursed by its mother for six to twelve weeks, before it becomes an independent member of the domestic flock.

The Arabian Camel *(Camelus dromedarius)* is only found in its domesticated state today, and has been used as a pack animal for over 5 000 years in desert and arid lands. The baby will stay with its mother for four years.

Furry babies

Most of us smile with pleasure and show great affection to a furry mammal nursing its young. No other class of animals lavishes so much care and attention upon its babies, often spending months and even years caring for the growing youngster until it is capable of looking after itself.

Mammals are defined as being warm-blooded animals which suckle their young. This means that there is contact of the closest kind between a mother mammal and her offspring, which on being born are entirely dependent on their mother for food in the form of milk until they are able to eat similar food to that of their parents. It is not surprising that a physical and emotional bond grows between the mother and offspring, and is one of the strongest emotional bonds to be found in the whole animal kingdom. Baby mammals also rely on their mother and sometimes their father for warmth and protection, and, usually, there is a long period of 'childhood' which allows the youngster to develop and mature while learning the tricks of survival in its highly competitive wildlife world.

Within a few minutes of birth, some baby mammals are able to walk, and to cope with their new surroundings. Baby antelopes, Giraffes *(Giraffa camelopardalis)*, elephants and horses can walk about within hours of birth. Other baby mammals are blind, naked and entirely helpless at birth. Polar Bear *(Thalarctos maritimus)* cubs weigh only about 310 grams (11 ounces) at birth and are blind and almost helpless. A newborn rabbit is also blind and with few hairs at birth. The mother in these cases has to spend much time feeding, caring, grooming and protecting the babies. It is possible to look at mammal groups and see the contrast between naked, helpless babies and those that are well developed and capable of walking. In the carnivore group, which includes the Lions, Tigers *(Panthera tigris)*, bears, dogs and foxes, most babies are born blind, naked and helpless, while in the hoofed mammals or ungulates,

Almost too big to cling to its mother's body, a young slow loris and mother are caught by flashlight on a nocturnal foray, hunting for insects and small lizards.

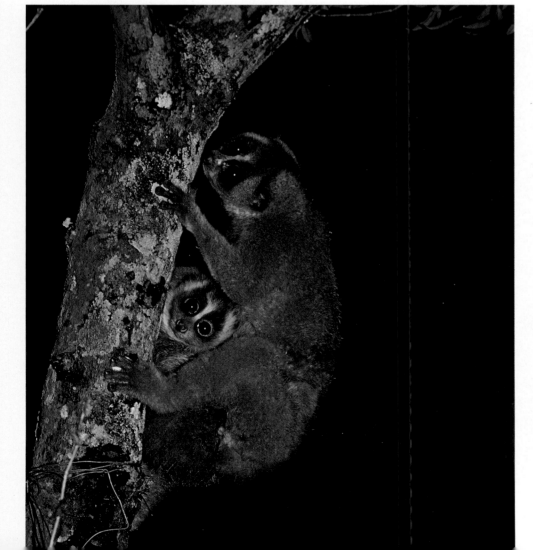

which includes the zebras, horses, antelopes, deer and Giraffes, the young struggle to their feet within minutes of birth and are soon tottering around and suckling from their mother, as well as moving with the feeding herd. The reason why there is such a difference is explained if the way of life of the two groups is examined.

Let us look at the life of a carnivore, the red fox, and then look at the life of an ungulate, such as a zebra. In the red fox, the male and females lead separate lives for most of the year, hunting on their own and taking little interest in other red foxes. With the onset of the breeding season, however, they meet and form pairs. The female fox or vixen prepares a nursery burrow in their earth and lines it with soft grasses and sometimes her own fur. She lies here to give birth to her babies, which usually number four or five. They are blind, naked and completely dependent on her for warmth, protection and milk. The vixen depends on her mate to bring

her food at this time, but the dog fox is careful not to enter right into the nursery, since this will produce aggression from the vixen. The babies are born in late winter, usually, and search out one of their mother's six teats which are on the underside of her body as in all mammals. She lies in a comfortable position while they suckle. At this stage all the babies do is suckle, rest and sleep as their eyes do not open until they are nine or ten days old. They gradually begin to be more active, and start exploring their nursery and then the earth. It is not until they are about five weeks old that they first poke their noses out of the earth's entrance and take a look at the outside world. At this stage they are most attractive bundles of sandy red fur. The next few weeks are spent exploring the immediate surroundings, then going with their mother on hunting trips and learning how to catch their own food. They are independent at about five months when they scatter to find their own hunting grounds.

Above
A young Zebra, like most grazing
mammalian babies, stands on its feet
within an hour of birth and is capable of
keeping up with its mother within a day
or so. This is a most important
requirement, as many predators, such as
Lions, are on the look-out for a weak
youngster for an easy meal.

Left
These five-day-old hedgehog youngsters,
with wrinkled faces and spines beginning
to harden, will open their eyes in about
nine days time.

Right
At birth, young rabbits are blind and
naked and are completely dependent on
their mother for warmth, protection and
food.

When the childhood of a red fox is compared with that of a zebra, there is a remarkable contrast. This hoofed mammal female usually has a single baby, unlike the fox's litter of several babies, and the zebra is born fully developed, with a full coat of hair, eyes open and ears pricked. After freeing itself from the birth sac which enclosed it during its 370-day development period, the foal instinctively tries to stand on its shaky legs and succeeds within a short time. It feeds from the mother's teats and is ready to move off with her within an hour or two. The mother is usually eager to rejoin the herd which she temporarily left in order to give birth to her baby. Although the foal stays near its mother it requires far less care and attention than the red fox cubs. The reason for this difference is related to the different feeding habits of the two groups. The red fox and most of its other carnivore relatives, are hunters and they have a home base where the young can be left while the parents hunt for food for the family. Often, they return with a freshly killed animal that will provide food for a day or even longer. The zebra and its hoofed relatives, however, feed on plant material and are usually social animals, living in herds. They are continually on the move looking for new vegetation to eat and they are often in the position of being hunted by carnivores, such as Lions or Leopards *(Panthera pardus)*. Therefore, the herd cannot remain in one place for any length of time, and the babies must be able to keep up with the running herd, escaping from danger.

Other mammals that are helpless at birth include hedgehogs, rabbits, mice, tree shrews, and badgers. In most of these it is the female who has the full responsibility of bringing up the babies. The father in the hedgehog family has long since wandered off to live alone when the female, or sow, gives birth to between three and seven youngsters in early summer. They are blind, probably deaf because their small ears are folded over, and their spines-to-be are no more than two patches of soft spines on the back. They do know, however, where to find milk and start to grow very quickly. The spines develop and soon harden and the little babies look more like adult hedgehogs. By the time they are one month old they can roll up in a ball, just like their mother does, when anything upsets them.

Baby rabbits are also blind, naked and virtually helpless at birth, but unlike the mother hedgehogs and fox vixen, the doe rabbit does not stay with her offspring all the time giving them her undivided attention. The pregnant doe digs her own nursery burrow which is a short burrow off the main tunnel of her warren. She prepares a soft bed

Above
A four-day-old red deer fawn waits patiently for the return of its mother. The tan coat with pale dappling helps to hide the baby from predators.

Far right
A young hare at birth is fully furred and has its eyes open and is soon ready to feed itself. Here, it is washing itself to keep its fur clean and in good condition.

for her babies from dry grass and her own fur, which she pulls from her body. The father or buck rabbit is totally unreliable and the doe does not let him near the new-born babies, as he may kill them. The doe does not stay with her babies all the time, but always covers the tunnel entrance with grass as she leaves. She does not stay away for very long, returning at frequent intervals to let them suckle from her. After about ten to fifteen days, the eyes and ears are open and the bodies are covered with soft fur. They soon begin to explore and in a few days appear at the entrance to the burrow. They begin to nibble grass and leaves and are quite independent. By this time their mother is probably expecting another litter of baby rabbits.

The mother hare is also an absentee parent but her babies are strikingly different. The mother gives birth to two to four babies which are called leverets. They are born with their eyes open and a full covering of soft fur. They can use their legs almost immediately, and look very attractive. The mother hare gives birth to them above ground, as hares do not burrow like rabbits. She then places each leveret in its own 'form' which is a concealed depression in long grass. She visits them in turn to allow them to suckle and spends the rest of her time feeding (mainly at dusk and dawn and during the hours of darkness) and sleeping. Why rabbit and hare mothers leave their babies for such a long time still puzzles zoologists. One of the most important things a mother mammal provides her babies with apart from a milk supply, is the warmth of her body. This is because in the early life of many mammal babies the mechanism that regulates their body temperature at a steady level is not working. It appears that the baby rabbits and leverets are able to regulate their temperatures better than most baby mammals and so can do without mother's warmth for long periods.

A baby that only gets fed every forty-eight hours was discovered just a few years ago. The adult animals were known but their babies had never been studied. This is the tree shrew which lives in the tropical forests of south-east Asia. It is a squirrel-like mammal, believed to be a primitive kind of primate. Tree shrews live in pairs and the mother builds a nursery nest for her babies. Two or three young are born and weigh about 14 grams (0·5 ounce). They are blind and deaf with a sparse covering of hair, but can survive for a very long time without mother. When their mother comes to let them suckle they take in so much that their stomachs become swollen and they look pot-bellied. This supply of high-protein, high-fat milk is enough to nourish them for the next forty-eight hours when mother next visits her babies.

As has been mentioned, most hoofed mammals are up on their feet and off with mother within a few hours of birth. In some deer, however, the young fawn is left alone for many hours. In the Red Deer (*Cervus elaphus*), the mother leaves the herd to have her baby in a quiet place such as soft, green bracken. She licks her young fawn clean after the

A brush-tailed possum baby attached to a teat in its mother's pouch. Marsupials are born at an embryonic stage of development and use their strong front limbs to drag themselves from the birth canal to the mother's pouch.

birth and as it dries, the spotted coat can be seen. This is very important for the survival of the baby. Most mammals are colour-blind and only see things in monochrome tones, just as we see things on a black-and-white television. The spotted fawn, lying quite still in its birthplace, is camouflaged by its coat, which resembles the dappling of light and shadow that passes through the ferns and plants around it. In addition, the fawn does not smell as its body scent organs are not functioning for the first few days of its life. It is, therefore, hidden from predators and the mother can go off for hours at a time to feed.

The most underdeveloped mammals at birth are found in Australia and South America. One group is the primitive Australasian monotremes, which lay eggs like their reptilian ancestors and birds. The Duck-billed Platypus *(Ornithorhynchus anatinus)* of eastern Australia spends much of its time swimming in slow streams and retreats to an underground network of burrows to sleep or escape from danger. The pregnant Platypus lays one or two tiny eggs (House-Sparrow size) on a

bed of soft grass and sits on them for about eleven days until they hatch. The babies are very tiny, about 25·4 millimetres (1 inch) long and they feed on the mother's milk. She does not have teats like other mammals but secretes milk from her milk glands on to her belly and the tiny Duck-billed Platypus baby laps it up. After about four months, when fully furred, the young emerge from the burrow. The other egg-layers are the spiny anteaters of Australia and New Guinea. The single egg is carried around by the mother in her pouch. When it hatches, about eleven days after being laid, the naked, blind baby feeds on milk secreted by the mother in the pouch.

The pouched mammals or marsupials of Australia and Central and South America give birth to young that look more like embryos than true babies. These tiny and immature youngsters, although blind and naked, are born with the knowledge of how to get from the birth opening between the mother's legs to the pouch. A marsupial's pouch is like a living cradle for the babies as they will rest here, feeding attached to one of the teats until they are developed enough to explore the world outside. The time the young spend in the pouch depends on the species.

The marsupials were the forerunners of the placental or true mammals and were once found throughout the world. It is believed that competition from the versatile true mammals killed off all the marsupials in Europe, Asia and North America, but they survived in Australia and South America because, as the true mammals evolved, these two continents were cut off from the rest of the world. However, there are still many different kinds of pouched mammals that are very similar to true mammals in their ways of life. There are marsupials that are cat-like, dog-like, mouse-like, mole-like and squirrel-like, as well as those that graze, climb trees and glide.

Probably the best known marsupials are the kangaroos and the Koalas *(Phascolarctos cinereus)*. The development of the Red Kangaroo *(Macropus rufus)* is well studied and is typical of marsupial breeding habits. About a month after mating, the female sits with her large hind legs open and a tiny baby Kangaroo is born from her cloacal or reproductive opening situated between the back legs. The baby weighs less than a gram (0·03 ounce) and is about 2 centimetres (0·8 inch) long.

A kangaroo with a half-grown joey surveying the world from the safety of its mother's pouch. It leaves the pouch to feed on the vegetation of its Australian bush home, but will dive back into the pouch at the least sign of danger.

It would easily fit in a teaspoon. Although it is blind with no hair and is generally poorly developed, the front limbs are quite well developed. Using these it scrambles and claws up a line of fur licked by the mother into the pouch and attaches itself to one of the four teats. It remains attached to this teat for several months until it is fully developed. It is about six to eight months later when the Kangaroo first puts out its head and looks around its living cradle. It is soon nibbling grass with its mother but at the first sign of danger it leaps headfirst into the safety of the pouch. There it squirms around until it can pop its head out and see the danger. Even when it is a year or so old the young joey, as it is called, will attempt to get into mother's pouch. However, it is now a tight squeeze and no doubt rather uncomfortable for mother, so when she has had enough she grabs hold of the joey's tail and flings it away.

Many marsupials, including the wombats, Koala and flying phalangers, give birth to only one baby at a time. These are among the larger pouched mammals. The smaller marsupials usually give birth to several babies, which squeeze into the mother's pouch. In America, the Common or Virginian Opossum (Didelphis virginiana) has sometimes given birth to more than twenty babies, but as she only has fourteen teats some are bound to die. On leaving the pouch the youngsters cling to their mother and hitch a free ride. They even attempt to do this when they are half the size of their mother, who is consequently laden down with offspring. A most attractive mother and baby is the Koala Bear and offspring, which always look very cuddly. However, this mum, like any mum, is very protective and aggressive and will strike out with powerful and sharp claws at anyone foolish enough to go too close.

Marsupials are not the only furry animals to carry their young. Many mammals will pick up their babies if the need arises and move them to a safer place or new home. Most wild cats and dogs will pick up their babies one by one by the scruff of the neck and carry them to a safer place if danger threatens. If the nest of a rodent such as a rat or mouse is disturbed, the small adult will busy itself moving its young. The beaver, a large rodent that builds dams and lodges in streams in Europe and

Top
Eight-week-old Virginian Opossums *(Didelphis virginiana)* riding on their mother's back. They are now fully developed and too large for her pouch.

Above
A mother Raccoon *(Procyon lotor)* carries her baby to a new safety area in the scrub of Arizona.

Far right
A young Koala *(Phascolarctos cinereus)* shares a meal of eucalyptus leaves with its mother. Quite often it will ride pickaback on its mother, feeding over her shoulder.

Overleaf
The Alpaca *(Lama pacos)* is important for its fine wool. The youngster suckles from its mother for six to twelve weeks, before becoming an independent member of the domestic flock.

A young baboon clings at first to its mother's chest, but soon learns to ride on her back 'jockey' style, going wherever mother travels.

America, will hold its offspring in its front arms and with its teeth, and walk erect. It can do this because it is designed to be able to stand on its back legs in order to cut down trees with its huge front teeth. Some placental mammals ride pickaback like marsupials. The babies of pangolins, and anteaters of South America, Sloth Bears *(Melursus ursinus)* and monkeys do this and make a most pleasing sight. A more unusual sight is a baby Hippopotamus *(Hippopotamus amphibius)* riding on its mother's back as she leisurely swims through her river or pool in Africa.

The young of the monkeys and baboons, that live in large social troops in Africa and Asia, hang on to mum in different positions as they grow older. At first a baby monkey will cling to its mother's belly with fingers and toes as she goes about her daily feeding behaviour with the rest of the troop. As it gets older it moves into a 'jockey' position, riding astride its mother's back as we do when riding a horse. When climbing a tree, a mother monkey is very agile and is able to use one arm

to cradle her infant so it does not fall from its clinging position. The various apes – Gorilla *(Gorilla gorilla)*, Orang-utan *(Pongo pygmaeus)*, Chimpanzee *(Pan troglodytes)* and gibbon – do this as well.

In the mammals that live an upside-down life the babies are provided with a living cradle. The three-toed sloths in their South American tropical jungle home spend almost their entire lives in one *Cecropia* tree and the baby clings to its mother's belly, being protected by the hanging arms and legs of its mother. The young of the flying phalangers of south-east Asia are provided with an even safer cradle. This strange mammal glides from tree to tree by using the webs of skin which extend from the sides of its chin right around the body, including fingers, toes and tail. When at rest the mother hangs upside-down and the baby rests within this natural cradle.

Many of the bats carry their babies for their first few days of life and this is indeed hazardous as bats are the only true fliers of the

A bat mother gives birth to a single offspring or twins. The baby instinctively clings to its mother's body and accompanies her on her flying trips. When it gets too heavy, the mother 'hangs up' her offspring in the roost while she goes hunting for food.

mammal world. The young bat clings tightly to its mother's body and goes wherever the mother goes. Later, the mother hangs her offspring up before flying off on a hunting expedition.

One of the most amusing mother and family scenes is found in certain species of shrew. Once her brood is active and walking the mother shrew sets off and all the babies 'follow-my-leader' as each youngster mouths a tuft of fur on the rear or tail of the one in front of it. The family search for earthworms and insects. One hot afternoon in late summer the author observed a family of five or six Stoats *(Mustela erminea)* zig-zagging their way across a six-lane road head to tail in a wavering 'train'.

Birth of a Thompson's Gazelle *(Gazella thomsoni)*. A mother lies on her side as the forefeet of her baby are pushed from the birth canal. This is soon followed by the rest of the baby and the mother immediately begins to eat the embryonic sac as it could attract predators. The next task is to lick her baby clean before it attempts to struggle to its feet and search for the mother's milk.

The length of time a baby takes milk from its mother varies from one kind of mammal to another. The giant of land mammals, the elephant, is the record holder, its baby suckling until the end of its second year. The elephant has the longest gestation period of all mammals, that of the African Elephant *(Loxodonta africana)* being about twenty-one months. Although an adult elephant drinks water by sucking up a large amount of liquid into its trunk and then squirting it into its mouth, the baby elephant has to learn how to use its trunk. To take its mother's milk it curls back its trunk and pushes its mouth up to one of her two teats, situated between her front legs. The life span of an elephant is very similar to man, the elephant maturing around fifteen years of age and living to the age of sixty or seventy. Most other mammals are weaned in a much shorter period of time, the majority of them within a few weeks.

In the wild, most mammalian mothers are able to cope with the birth and tending of babies with an efficiency which is quite astonishing. There are no 'baby' or prenatal classes, doctors, nurses or specialists to help with the birth, but most new

mothers seem to know exactly what to do – how to lick the baby clean immediately it has been born, how to feed it, often nudging it to the teats, and how to keep the baby clean. Maternal behaviour is to a great extent inborn or instinctive knowledge, which directs the behaviour of the majority of lower animals, the invertebrates and, to a great extent, the less advanced vertebrates. Even so, watching and learning from other females, if the mammals live in groups or social communities, is very important. In the wild, the Orang-utan, Gorilla, gibbon and Chimpanzee mothers are known to gain knowledge in child-rearing by seeing births and babies being cared for within the family group. In many monkey and baboon troops the same experience is gained. Incomplete success in breeding in captivity is often due to the lack of this learning process, resulting in the mother not knowing what to do with the wet baby she gives birth to. Sometimes she rejects the baby and occasionally even kills it. If the zoo attendants see this kind of behaviour from a mother, the baby is removed and reared by a keeper with feeding-bottles, in the same way as many human babies.

Above
The elephant baby is born after about twenty-one months gestation and takes its mother's milk until the end of its second year. It does not mature until around fifteen years of age.

Right
Chimpanzee *(Pan troglodytes)* mother and baby. The primates lavish much care and attention on their babies, ties being strong between parents and young.

Left
A Cheetah (*Acinonyx jubatus*) mother usually has to raise her cubs without the help of the male who has long since gone to lead his independent life. She will teach the cubs as they grow to stalk and sprint after prey.

Below
A young Lion (*Panthera leo*) cub grows up among its large family, learning the techniques of hunting from the adults of the pride.

Right
The Giraffe *(Giraffa camelopardalis)* normally has one young. The 2-metre-tall youngster is soon grouped with other babies and tended by an 'aunt' giraffe in a creche. This allows the other parents to concentrate on feeding, and then take turns in attending to the offspring.

Because it is the female that gives birth to and suckles the offspring, she is usually the one that bears the brunt of rearing the young. Male mammals often mate with several females or, occasionally, the female will mate with several males, and when the babies are born there are no family ties or known blood relationships. This is the case in hoofed mammals such as deer, zebras and antelopes, where there is no paternal care. However, in some mammals, such as in the fox or jackal, in which the father forms part of the family, he does do some work. Usually his main duty is getting food and bringing it back for the family. In some cases, however, the male takes over some of the duties of caring for baby, such as the small South American monkeys, the marmosets and tamarins, and the Siamangs *(Symphalangus syndactylus)*, small apes from south-east Asia. In marmosets, the mother usually bears twins but these are passed over to father soon after birth and they cling to his back, often being slung around his neck like a scarf. He passes them back to the mother only at feeding time. When the growing Siamang baby is weaned, the female appears to lose interest and the male takes over the responsibilities of the infant during the time of its life when it is learning to be independent.

It is not always just the parents that help with the rearing of the young in mammals. In a langur monkey population, all the females cluster round a new mother and take turns in handling the youngsters. This type of behaviour is usually called 'aunt behaviour'. There are aunties to be found in several kinds of mammals, especially where they live in social groups such as troops, flocks, herds and packs. It is believed that when young Giraffes

Playing 'king-of-the-castle' helps to
develop a young kid's sense of balance
and expertise in climbing mountains.

(Giraffa camelopardalis) and Hippopotamuses (Hippopotomus amphibus) reach a certain age they are looked after by adult 'aunties' and often the growing youngsters are kept together in a creche so that they can be more easily cared for.

Play is very important in young mammals because it is one way of learning and practising skills which are needed for adult life. The various kinds of flesh-eating youngsters have to learn all the tricks and techniques of hunting. As soon as they are old enough, they begin to stalk and fight their brothers, sisters and parents, pouncing on one another and attempting to climb trees. We have all seen a kitten or puppy chase its tail or pounce on a ball, but these acts of behaviour can be seen in their wild relatives such as Lion cubs, fox cubs and Badger babies (Meles meles). Their play activities

sometimes look quite ferocious as they grab at throats or rugby tackle each other, but they do not harm themselves. They instinctively know how far to go without breaking the skin of a sibling. Play also helps to train them in muscular control and precision. As they get older the babies of hunters accompany their parent or parents on hunting trips and learn about the real thing. They gradually become more expert in catching their own food and eventually are masters of hunting and can go off to lead independent lives. Sometimes they are chased away by the parents.

Although hoofed mammals can walk and run well within a few days of birth, they still play with one another in order to perfect their running and leaping abilities that will be so important when being chased by a hungry carnivore.

Alaskan Brown Bear (Ursus arctos) female still cares for her three cubs and watches over their activities, although they are now a year old and well on the way to being independent.

Young fawns of Red Deer and Fallow Deer (Dama dama) can be seen playing together, chasing one another round a mound or tree. Goat kids play king-of-the-castle on their parents back or on rocks and crags.

In some of the more intelligent mammal babies, behaviour is sometimes seen that does not seem to have the function of learning for adult life. For example, a Chimpanzee baby will amuse itself for minutes on end by dressing itself up with pieces of vagatation and turning somersaults over and over again. They are probably just having a good time and thoroughly enjoying themselves!

51

The water nursery

For most creatures in the aquatic world, the reproduction of their own kind is a comparatively simple matter. Male and female simply shed their sperm and eggs into the water, where they mix and meet one another in random fashion and fertilization occurs. This is the pattern that occurs in fresh water and sea water, in groups from aquatic worms, starfishes and sea urchins, to fishes such as mackerel, herring and carp. However, in nearly all the aquatic groups there are exceptions to be found and quite amazing methods of reproduction and care of the young occur.

Marine babies

The salty seas of the world is the environment that supported the first living creatures and it is still the home of millions of animals. The warm surface waters, full of oxygen and food, are a favoured home for thousands of baby sea animals. Many bottom-dwelling creatures ensure their babies are introduced into this environment to give them the best possible start in life. The millions upon millions of animals and plants which gather together as living specks in the surface waters are called plankton, meaning 'that which is made to wander'. About six-tenths of the plankton is made up of single-celled algae known as diatoms. The rest contains not only minute plants, but swarms of equally minute animal forms, representatives of almost every phylum of the animal kingdom, and includes tiny babies of thousands of kinds of fish. The young or larvae of flat worms, sea urchins, shore crabs, barnacles, limpets, starfish, brittle stars, copepods and sea squirts are just a few of the invertebrates that live and grow together in the plankton. Nearly all these larvae are tiny, translucent, jelly-like creatures which have fine hairs or cilia that they can move to help them stay up in the water. Although often distantly related, the larvae look far more like each other than their parents.

Some of the most beautiful larvae of the plankton are the larvae of starfish, brittle-stars, sea urchins, sand dollars and sea cucumbers, all of which belong to the large and widespread phylum Echinodermata. In most species, eggs and sperm are shed into the sea by the bottom-dwelling adults, where fertilization takes place. The fertilized eggs float up to the plankton and develop long arms, stiffened with rods. After floating for some time, the larvae develop into the adult form and sink slowly to the seabed and so begin their adult lives.

Crustaceans, such as crabs, shrimps and barnacles, also begin their lives in the plankton soon after hatching. A female crab or lobster usually carries her fertilized eggs in a mass under her curved tail segments and, as the larvae hatch, they float up to join the plankton. These youngsters are called nauplii larvae.

A barnacle is a crustacean leading an upside-down life inside a horny or calcareous case, using its legs to draw in minute food particles. They are glued to rocks or any object in

the sea, including whales. The barnacles begin their lives as planktonic larvae and have tiny pointed horns on the front of their carapace. They go through several changes and eventually drift inshore and rest on a rock or similar surface and glands glue the tiny animal to it.

The free-swimming, pulsating jellyfish have an interesting life cycle. The fertilized egg settles and grows into a creature that looks rather like a sea anemone, which gradually develops and makes many tiny sections, like plates piled up, across its body. These cut themselves off one by one and float away as miniature jellyfish or ephyrae and continue their development in the plankton. In spite of their fragility, they are ruthless predators and devour many kinds of larvae in the plankton.

Many fishes, including some which are important to Man as food, produce larvae that spend the first

A beautiful Beadlet Anemone *(Actinia equina)* with her newly budded young anemones, replicas of the adult animal.

few months of their lives in the plankton. Cod *(Gadus morrhua)*, mackerel, hake, Plaice *(Pleuronectes platessa)*, halibut and herring all produce defenceless young that develop in the rich soup of plankton. The parents gather in huge shoals in suitable localities and the individuals of both sexes shed their eggs and sperm into the water. The fertilized eggs are subsequently abandoned by the parents and left to the mercy of physical conditions. As in the other youngsters of the plankton we have mentioned, the babies are at the mercy of the winds and currents, many eggs are eaten by other fishes or other carnivorous sea creatures, many are killed by changes of temperature and other physical catastrophes, and many are thrown on the beach by strong currents. As a result the number of eggs produced is enormous in comparison with those which survive to become adult fish. It has been estimated that in the Cod less than one egg in every million released ever becomes an adult Cod. The eggs of a Cod hatch in fourteen to fifteen days and the larvae, 5 millimetres (0·2 inch) long feed on the food left in the attached yolk sacs. When they are about a week old they begin to devour other members of the plankton, favouring the crustacean

copepod larvae. At ten weeks old they are about 2 – 2·5 centimetres (0·8 – 1 inch) long and they begin to go down to feed on the seabed, in shallow coastal waters. They now eat small crustaceans and worms. Those that survive to be a year old are 15 – 18 centimetres (6 – 7 inches) long and can eat animals including other fish as long as themselves.

The development of young flatfish is particularly interesting. Plaice, Sole *(Solea solea)* and other flatfish begin life as floating eggs which hatch into tiny fish larvae 5 millimetres (0·2 inch) long. They feed at first on diatoms and by the time they are six to eight weeks old they have doubled their length and are eating larger plankton prey. They then sink down, settle on the seabed and start to lie on one side. In Plaice, this is usually the left side. Gradually, as the fish grows, the left eye migrates over the top of the head towards the right side and the mouth twists. The upper side darkens with pigments while the hidden left side remains pale. The side-to-side movements of the planktonic baby fish now become up-and-down movements, and the fish leads a typical adult flatfish life.

Certain fish spend their adult lives in fresh water but use the sea as a nursery. Well-known examples

Above
A young fry of a flatfish is symmetrical and a typical 'herring' fish shape. As it settles on the sea bed it lies on one side (usually the left side) and the eye on this side slowly migrates over the top of the head to the upper side. The original ventral fins of this American plaice are facing towards us in this photograph.

Right
Young eels hatch in the Sargasso Sea of the western Atlantic Ocean and are known as leptocephalus larvae. They reach European or American freshwater rivers by slowly drifting with the currents and change into transparent elvers. They swim upstream and remain there for several years.

are the American Eel *(Anguilla bostoniensis)* and European Eel *(Anguilla anguilla)*. The adults journey from European and American rivers and streams down to the sea and swim all the way to their breeding grounds in the Sargasso Sea in the western Atlantic Ocean. The fertilized eggs hatch into flat, leaf-like transparent larvae known as leptocephalus larvae. These young drift in the ocean currents and arrive in western European and Mediterra-

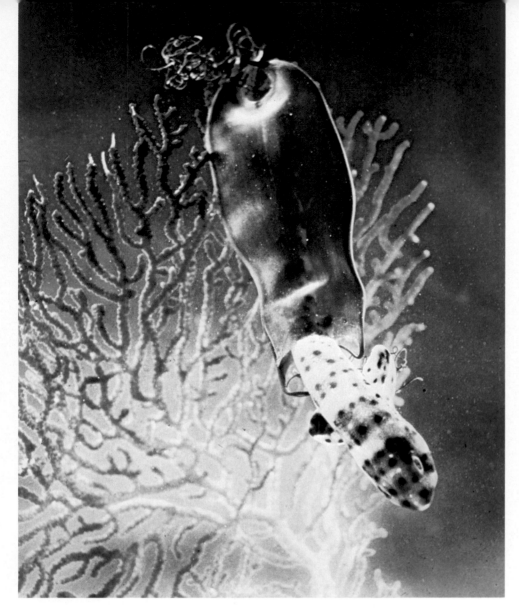

nean waters three years later, and off the north-western Atlantic coast of America about one year later. They transform themselves into thin, cylindrical eels which are still transparent and are known as elvers. On entering these waters their bodies change to deal with the freshwater environment. They spend several years in fresh water, maturing until they are ready to breed and start their long migratory journeys. New Zealand Whitebait *(Galaxias attenuatus)* also lay their eggs at sea but spend their adult lives in the fast-flowing streams of the islands.

Several of the larger species of cartilaginous fish – the sharks, rays and dogfish – give birth to live young. These include the blue sharks, hammerhead sharks and man-eating Great White Shark *(Carcharodon carcharias)*. Many of the smaller species of skates, rays and dogfish lay a small number of eggs, each one protected by a tough horny textured shell or flattened, oblong envelope. As well as the egg, the envelope contains a certain amount of semi-fluid albuminous (egg-white) material. The four corners are usually drawn out so that the tendril can become coiled around pieces of

Above
A fully developed dogfish struggles free from its mermaid's purse, the leathery egg case in which it developed.

Right
Young Green Turtles *(Chelonia mydas)* have successfully reached the warm waters from their sandy shore nest, but many dangers still threaten. They may be eaten by predatory fishes, birds and other marine creatures, with only two or three surviving from the dozens that emerge from each nest.

Far right
A Harp Seal *(Pagophilus greenlandicus)* mother with her attractive, white-coated pup. The white coat moults after about ten days and the pup has a grey spotted coat. 'White coats' are killed in thousands for their skins, although efforts are being made to stop the slaughter of these defenceless youngsters.

algae or other fixed object which serves as an anchor to the egg during its development, which lasts from four-and-a-half to sixteen months depending on the species. Finally, the little fish makes its escape through a slit in one end of the capsule. The capsules have been given many names including 'sailor's purses', 'mermaid's purses', and 'mermaid's pin-boxes'. They are sometimes found cast up by the tide on a seashore.

Although the majority of the bony fish that live in the wide open oceans and seas of the world just scatter thousands of eggs into the seas and leave them to fend for themselves, a few species do show some parental care of their young. Several inshore fishes lay a smaller number of eggs and look after them to some degree. Many of the gobies, blennies, bullheads, sculpins and clingfishes deposit their eggs in cracks, crevices or in dead shells of bivalves for safety. The male often mounts guard and, in some sculpins, clasps the eggs between his paired fins, so brooding them in a fashion. The Gunnel or Butterfish *(Pholis gunnellus)* rolls its eggs into a ball, the size of a brazil nut and remains coiled around them until they

hatch. The kelpfish, a type of blenny that lives in Caribbean waters, lays its eggs inside living sponges. The young fish stay for a while inside the sponge, feeding on small plankton brought in with the currents of water drawn in by the sponge.

The warmer waters of the oceans are the home of the baby turtles. These reptilian youngsters hatch from leathery eggs, which their mother lays in sandy beaches just above the high-tide line, after developing for seven to ten weeks. The hatchlings have to fight their way to the surface of the sand and usually emerge at night when it is cooler and there are not as many enemies around. They instinctively know the direction of the sea and 'paddle' strongly with their tiny flippers over the sand to reach the water. This fairly short journey down the shore is very hazardous for the babies as many are snapped up by ghost crabs, snakes, gulls, frigate birds and Dholes *(Cuon javanicus)*. Even Tigers have been known to eat them. On reaching the sea they swim for deeper waters but even then, the majority are eaten by fish.

Seals and sealions leave the oceans once a year for the birth of

the baby seals or pups. This may be to a rocky or sandy shore such as in the Grey Seal *(Halichoerus grypus)* and Common Seal *(Phoca vitulina)*, or on ice as in the Harp Seal *(Pagophilus greenlandicus)* and Weddell Seal *(Leptonychotes weddelli)*. The babies have been developing inside their mother for eight to twelve months and usually the mother gives birth to a single pup, twins being quite rare. All the newborn pups are able to swim at birth, but most species need to fatten themselves up with blubber which gives them buoyancy and protects them from the cold waters, and this takes several weeks. However, they grow rapidly during their nursing period because the mother's milk is particularly rich, being about 50 per cent fat. Some of the seal pups are most attractive because they are covered with white, woolly coats. In the Harp Seal this is very important for the pup. Its white coat, apart from keeping it warm, helps to camouflage it on the ice when the mother leaves it to go off to feed. A young Harp Seal moults after twenty to twenty-six days and gets its adult coat. Soon after this it enters the sea and feeds, at first, mainly on small crustaceans.

Right
Four-day-old salmon alevins still carrying the remnant of their yolk sac. When the yolk sac is used up they will begin to feed on diatoms and tiny freshwater crustaceans.

Top
A young Southern Right Whale *(Eubalaena australis)* mother and her calf photographed from the air off the coast of Argentina, South America. A female whale usually migrates to warm waters to give birth to her single offspring, so that the baby stands a better chance of survival.

Above
Sea Otter *(Enhydra lutris)* mother and her week-old pup. The pup is usually born on shore but is soon in its aquatic home, resting, feeding and sleeping on its mother's belly.

The attractive Sea Otter *(Enhydra lutris)* of Pacific waters leaves its ocean home only for a brief period to give birth to its single pup. The pup is well-developed at birth with its eyes open, its full set of milk teeth and a coat of fur. The mother immediately carries her pup into the water and gives it constant and careful attention, nursing and grooming it on her chest as she swims or floats along on her back. The pup stays with her for a year or more during which time it is taught the expertise of hunting food, such as sea urchins, clams, crabs and mussels, as well as the occasional fish or octopus.

Whales and dolphins are mammals that give birth at sea and, like the seals, usually give birth to one young. The baby develops inside its mother for quite a long time, between eleven and sixteen months depending on the species. At birth the baby is quite large, usually between one-quarter and one-third its mother's length. For example, a Blue Whale mother of 23 metres (77

feet) in length gives birth after ten or eleven months gestation to a calf that is about 7·5 metres (25 feet) long. The length of the calf doubles during the six- to seven-month period of suckling.

Immediately after being born the baby whale or dolphin must reach the surface of the water for a supply of air. It has been observed that dolphin mothers push the baby up to the surface and this probably happens in all the various species. The mother floats on her side so the youngster can suckle and breathe at the same time. Later the baby learns to nurse under water. The mother's teats lie within paired slits on either side of the reproductive opening. The mother can contract certain body muscles and force milk from her mammary glands via the teats into the mouth of the young. All dolphin and whale calves grow rapidly and this is partly due to the high calcium and phosphorus content of the milk.

There are certain sea-dwelling fishes that leave the oceans to travel

up freshwater rivers and streams in order to produce young. The most famous of these are the salmon. The breeding season for the Atlantic Salmon *(Salmo salar)* extends from September to February but these fish approach the coasts and enter rivers every month of the year. The Salmon stop feeding on entering fresh water and journey up the rivers, gradually losing weight. So great is the urge for reproduction that they struggle up rapids and jump weirs and waterfalls until they reach the spawning grounds in the head streams. On arrival they pair and the female scoops out a shallow depression in gravelly shallows with her tail and body. The pair then spawn, the fertilized eggs sink and, being slightly sticky, adhere to the bottom. The female loosely covers the eggs and they are left to develop without any further attention from the exhausted parents, the majority of which die on their return journey to the sea.

The Salmon eggs hatch in five to twenty-one weeks depending on the temperature and are about 12 millimetres (0·5 inch) long and are called alevins. They feed on the remains of their yolk-sac and in four to eight weeks are 25 – 60 millimetres (1 – 2·4 inches) long and are called fingerlings. They live in shallow water and feed on small aquatic animals. At the end of a year they have doubled their size and are called parrs. During their second year they develop ten or eleven dark bands on each side of the body which look like thumbmarks. In the next few years (although this can take place in a year) they become silvery and look rather like a trout. They are known as smoult and are ready for their journey to the sea where they will spend their adult life before returning to their birthplace to spawn. Other fish that leave the sea to reproduce their young in fresh water include the Sea Lamprey, *(Petromyzon marinus)*, Sturgeon *(Acipenser sturio)*, shad, and Sea Trout *(Salmo trutta)*.

Freshwater babies

The hazards and benefits of growing up in fresh water are similar to the ocean nursery environment. There is freshwater plankton for the developing babies to feed on. It consists of tiny plants such as desmids, diatoms and filamentous algae, and minute animals such as crustaceans, rotifers and insect larvae. There are fewer invertebrate larvae in freshwater plankton than in marine plankton. Most freshwater creatures tend to lay large, yolky eggs attached to water plants or stones and the larvae are well developed on hatching. Fairy shrimps, back swimmers, water fleas and copepods are all crustaceans that live in the plankton. Water flea females can produce offspring without mating and all these babies are females. In fact, if the water is warm and there is a lot of food, a female water flea can be a grandmother before her offspring are born. This is because the babies developing inside her body

Right
A minute female freshwater water flea with her greenish eggs clearly visible through her semi-transparent shell.

Below
The larva of a caddisfly encases itself with grains of sand, weeds, pebbles or tiny shells (seen here). The case protects the developing larva as well as holding it down on the stream bed, while the head and limbs emerge to move and feed.

Far right
A dragonfly emerges from its pupa. After many months as a voracious carnivorous larva, this insect pupates briefly before emerging as a dazzlingly beautiful adult.

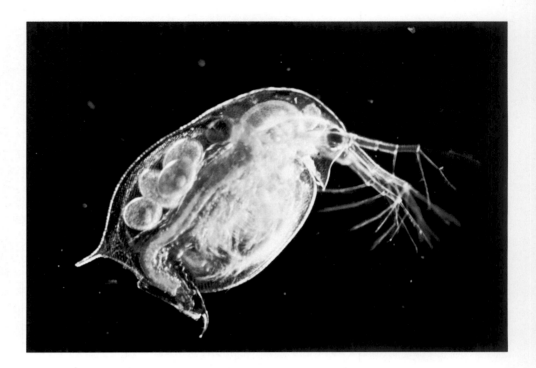

are already producing female babies inside their bodies. Later in the summer both males and females appear and they mate normally, giving rise to resistant eggs which can survive harsh conditions, such as the winter months and the pond drying up.

Many insects that fly in the air in adult form, require fresh water for breeding. One of these is the mosquito, of which there are many species to be found around the world. After mating in the air, the female lays her eggs on the surface or vegetation of the water. When the eggs hatch, the larvae look more like worms than flies. They have a segmented body with a tufted tail and a hollow tube (siphon) at the rear end and a large head with a pair of dark eyes at the other. Normally the larva hangs down from the water surface, its siphon piercing the surface film and functioning as a breathing tube. The larva moults at intervals and eventually on the fifth moult changes into a pupa. This is bulky, with a round head and thorax combined. Although it does not feed, it is active for the few days of the pupal stage. In the last stages of its pupal life it rises to the surface of the water, its hard outer skin splits and the adult mosquito pulls itself out and soon takes to the air to find a mate.

The stream bed makes a splendid environment for many insect larvae. It is the home of the larvae or nymphs of stoneflies, caddisflies, mayflies and alderflies. The nymphs spend months and sometimes years on the bottom, feeding on other creatures. The caddisfly larvae have conical tubular cases made from tiny pebbles, grasses, minute shells or similar local materials. This mobile home gives the larva protection and camouflage as well as holding the creature down on the stream bed. The front end of the case is open and the larva can have its head, thorax and three pairs of legs hanging out. It can move quite freely, dragging its case behind, feeding on either plant or animal material depending on the species. When it is ready to pupate it seals itself in, after anchoring the case to the stream bed, and a few weeks later an incomplete adult caddisfly called a subimago emerges, makes for the surface and splits its skin so that the adult fly or imago can emerge.

The mayfly larvae spend three or four years on the stream bed, feeding mainly on algae. They are quite brightly coloured and have three tail spines. When it is time, they climb out of the water and the fully grown larvae moult, first into subimagos, incomplete adults with wing buds, and then into adults.

A fierce predator of streams and quieter stretches of rivers and lakes is the offspring of the beautiful dragonflies and damsonflies. After mating the female dips over the water's surface and lays her eggs there. Within three to four weeks tiny larvae or nymphs hatch that immediately begin to prey on small water animals, often smaller larvae of other species. They grow rapidly and become efficient hunters of tadpoles and even fish such as sticklebacks and minnows larger than themselves. To catch prey, the nymph holds on to a stone or plant with its three pairs of clawed legs and aligns itself with its moving

prey. Then it shoots out its extensible lower lip called the labium or mask, which is armed with pincers. The pincers grab the prey and bring it back to the jaws which then take over the job of devouring the victim. Although the larvae do eat young baby fishes, they do quite a lot of good by devouring great numbers of mosquito larvae. When fully grown, after two or more years, the lava pupates briefly on a stem out of water and then splits the case so that a beautiful adult can emerge. The wings are extended by liquid being pumped into the veins by the fat body.

Most freshwater fishes, as with marine fishes, lay eggs and take no further interest. However, some take elaborate care of their young and often it is the duty of the male fish. Many species, such as the cichlids, Jack Dempsey *(Cichlasoma biocellatus)* and Jewelfish *(Hemichromis bimaculatus)*, dig nursery

pits for the young. Both parents guard the eggs and as soon as the larvae hatch they are watched over to prevent any active ones straying. If they do swim off, they are sucked carefully into the adult's mouth and blown out into the nursery pit. Later the larvae move in a shoal following their parents, the colour patterns apparently being the key factor. When they are strong and self-supporting they disperse. Many of the colourful cichlid fishes first protect their eggs by carrying them in their mouths and, by gulping in water, ensure a perfect oxygen supply as well as their safety. This duty is usually undertaken by the female and the young fry hatch inside her mouth and do not leave it. Later they venture from this shelter but do not stray far, keeping always within reach of her head. At the least threat of danger they rapidly return to their refuge. A unique form of parental care is shown by a

Above
A freshwater Crayfish *(Astacus pallipes)* female held in the hand to show her developing eggs under the abdomen's tail. On hatching, the young cling here, and on the bristles of her legs and abdomen until ready to feed and lead independent lives.

Right
The fry of South American Discus Fish *(Symphysodon discus)* stay close to their parent's body for three to four weeks, apparently attracted by the secretions of the skin on which they feed.

South American cichlid, the Discus or Pompadour Fish *(Symphysodon discus)*. Both parents allow their newly hatched youngsters to feed on the mucus covering their bodies, and the adults flick the brood from one to another. In aquarium-kept Discus Fish this behaviour lasts six weeks.

Life cycle of a frog. The female frog sheds her eggs, thinly-coated with jelly, which are fertilized as they leave her body by the male clinging to her back (amplexus). The jelly swells on contact with water to form the familiar frog spawn *(far left)*. On hatching the tadpoles live on a small reserve of yolk from the egg, breathing through the three pairs of feathered external gills *(left)*. The external gills are soon lost and the tadpoles breathe through internal gills, like fish, and their skin. The hind limbs grow at around six weeks, soon followed by the front limbs *(below left)*. The tadpole begins to be recognizable as a frog. It now has lungs and will gulp in air at the pond's surface *(below)*.

Above
A Canadian Beaver *(Castor canadensis)* attending to her kit in shallow water. Two to four babies are born inside the lodge and soon emerge to accompany their mother on her trips for food and building materials.

Right
A young Hippopotamus *(Hippopotamus amphibius)* nuzzles up to its mother, who usually gives birth to her baby on land. The youngster can walk, run and swim within five minutes of birth.

Male Siamese Fighting Fish *(Betta splendens)* are renowned for their aggression but their breeding habits are also noteworthy. The male builds a raft of bubbles and then courts a female ready to spawn. He wraps himself around her body and as the eggs are laid he fertilizes them, catches them in his mouth and puts them in his raft. The male takes complete charge, driving his mate away. The young usually hatch in thirty-six hours and are swimming freely within three days. The male then loses interest and leaves the young to care for themselves.

The majority of frogs, toads, newts and salamanders are amphibians that must return to water for their young to be born and mature into adults. Their spawn is well known in ponds and streams, the eggs being protected by gelatinous jelly. The young tadpoles grow through the summer months developing through various stages until a miniature adult is formed. In the Common Frog this takes sixteen weeks, after which it can climb on to land to continue its growth.

There are no totally aquatic, freshwater mammals. Young otters are born in a den close to water and are soon playing and diving in it. The beaver young or kits, however, are born on a platform just above the surface of the water. This is because their home is inside a lodge built from cut branches and mud in a stream dammed by the adults. The lodge has a resting platform constructed inside it and the beavers enter by submerged passages. Although a kit is only 0·45 kilograms (1 pound) at birth, it is fully developed with its eyes open, and by four weeks it can find its own aspen and willow bark to eat.

A large mammal of fresh water is the African Hippopotamus *(Hippopotamus amphibius)*. The female usually bears her single young on shore but cases are known where the birth has occurred in water. This baby can walk, run or swim within five minutes of birth.

Babies
in nests

A male Three-spined Stickleback *(Gasterosteus aculeatus)* still in his bright breeding colours keeping a watchful eye over a week-old baby.

Babies that are born in nests usually gain a certain amount of protection from predators, as well as warmth from the nest materials and the adult that sits on them. A great variety of nests have evolved in the animal kingdom to protect and insulate the young to some degree.

It is birds that we immediately think of as being the master builders of nests but there are many examples to be found in the rest of the animal kingdom, particularly in the vertebrates. A few nest builders have already been mentioned in the preceding chapters, such as rabbits, otters, and Siamese Fighting Fish. In the fishes the best-known and best-studied nest builder is the stickleback. There are several species, all of which build nests. The males construct the nest from water weeds and other plant material, cementing the pieces together with a sticky substance secreted from their kidneys. When the nest is finished the male courts a gravid female with a zig-zag dance, leading her to his hollow tube, nudging her to enter and lay her eggs. Then he enters and fertilizes them immediately. The female is chased away and the male, in his breeding colours of blue eye and red belly, looks for another female. When several hundred eggs have been laid, the male stands guard throughout the incubation period of eight to twelve days, continually fanning currents of water over the developing eggs to aerate them. He guards the hatchlings for the first few days of their lives before they disperse. Within their first year the young sticklebacks grow from 4 millimetres (0·16 inch) to 4 centimetres (1·6 inch), reaching their adult length of about 6 centimetres (2·4 inches) in their second year.

Another family of reptiles, apart from the turtles which have already been mentioned, build nests and guard them during the breeding season, the alligator and crocodile family. Its members are semi-aquatic and during the breeding season they select territories for themselves and squabble over nesting space. The female digs a pit or constructs a small mound of mud and vegetation, in which she lays her soft leathery eggs after mating with a male, who has guarded the nesting territory. The female then guards her nest but does not sit on the eggs to incubate them as does a bird. The heat of the sun and the warmth given out by the rotting vegetation of the nest incubates the eggs. As they hatch it has been observed that the small squeals given out by the newborn, stimulate the mother to scrape away at the nest to help them escape. Mother then leaves the completely developed young to fend for themselves. Many babies are eaten by hungry carnivorous mammals and birds and even parent alligators or crocodiles.

Although most snakes abandon their eggs as soon as they are laid the King Cobra *(Ophiophagus hannah)* of south-east Asia builds quite a large nest and the mated pair watch over it. The female often coils around her twenty-four to thirty-six eggs which helps to keep them at a constant temperature during their development. Certain other female snakes, including pythons, coil

Below
Smooth Green Snakes *(Opheadrys vernalis)* of America hatching from their leathery shells. These snakes have a very short incubation period which may end in a few days and never lasts more than twenty-three days. Obviously, the development takes place largely before the eggs are laid.

Bottom
Baby freshwater crocodiles recently emerged from their eggs, ready to begin feeding. They grow rapidly reaching adult size in two to three years.

around their eggs to protect them and stabilize the temperature.

The most professional nest built by a mammal is without doubt that of the Harvest Mouse *(Micromys minutus)* which lives in Europe and Asia, inhabiting pastures and fields of cereal crops. Unfortunately this most attractive 13-centimetre (5-inch) long mammal is not as numerous as it used to be over parts of its range, due to agricultural methods such as the use of reaping machines and earlier harvesting. The female breeds from April to September and her first task is to construct the nest. It is a round nest about 8 centimetres (3 inches) in diameter, woven of grass or cereal blades split down their length. The nest is woven so that two or three stalks of the growing vegetation support it above the ground. There is no definite opening, the nest material being pushed aside for an entrance and exit. Inside the small nest the female gives birth to between five and nine naked, blind and tiny babies after

twenty-one days gestation. At eight days the babies open their eyes and are covered with fur, and they begin to poke their heads outside their nest. Three days later they start to explore the outside, gripping tightly to stalks with their hands and feet, helped by their prehensile tails. Another four or five days later they are independent, but do not take on the reddish tint of the adult until the end of the year. The mother will produce several litters in a season.

The other notorious nest builder in the mammals is the squirrel. The Grey Squirrel *(Sciurus cardinensis)* makes a domed nest, called a drey, from twigs. It is a rather clumsy, untidy structure, wedged in a tree fork high above the ground. It lines the drey with grass and leaves and this is usually the summer home. Usually, the young Grey Squirrels are born in a nest hidden in a hollow tree. The young, called kittens, are born in early spring, a second litter often following at the beginning of summer.

Above
Red squirrel babies, a few days old, nestle in their nest of sticks on a bed of soft mosses and lichens.

Right
Hazel Dormice *(Muscardinus avellanarius)* at home. These agile rodents construct their nest in the undergrowth of the deciduous woodlands of Europe and Asia Minor.

Overleaf
Eagle owls lay their eggs in unlined depressions on the ground. These are young Cape Eagle Owls *(Bubo capensis mackinderi)*.

Without doubt the experts of nests are the birds and all birds need some form of nest in which to lay their eggs. This does not mean that a nest is always built as some birds use natural occurrences. A cliff ledge is an ideal situation for the nest of a Guillemot *(Uria aalge)* and the eggs are conical to prevent them rolling off when the adult bird leaves its incubation task to go off to have a quick feed. Another example is the Little Tern *(Sterna albifrons)*, which uses a little depression on a pebbly beach. Perhaps the most fascinating nest site for laying an egg is that of its relative, the Fairy Tern *(Gygis alba)*, which lays its single egg in a small hollow on a tree branch. The chick has small, curved claws with which it hangs on tight when born. Surprisingly, there is a high rate of success of rearing Fairy Tern babies!

Each species of bird instinctively knows what kind of a nest to build. Ducks, geese, and many other birds that nest in damp and cold places, make fairly simple nests but ensure that they are thick enough to give adequate insulation for the brooding bird, eggs and chicks. Most female ducks and geese add a further insulating layer of down. The most famous duck to do this is the Eider Duck *(Somateria mollissima)* of rocky and sandy coasts from the Arctic to northern Europe, the nest being a fluffy mass of speckled down. The graceful swans pile up their heaps of plant material, throwing branches sideways and often extending their nest each year so that it becomes enormous.

Large, tree nesting birds, such as rooks, pigeons and herons, use rigid twigs and rely on height for safety. Herons build a platform of sticks at the top of a tree. Pigeons make an untidy thin platform, the bird's bill quivering when each twig is put in place to work it into the existing structure. The Bullfinch *(Pyrrhula pyrrhula)* builds a rather ragged nest in a thick hedge of fine projecting twigs, but the inside is lined with an almost separate cup of fine rootlets and hair to protect the eggs and chicks when they hatch. The cup-shaped nest is the most common type, but there are many variations and quite complicated nests may be found. The Magpie *(Pica pica)* builds a domed nest as does the tiny Wren *(Troglodytes troglodytes)* and water-loving dippers. Some birds use spider's webs in their nest-building activities. The Chaffinch *(Fringilla coelebs)* uses gossamer for its cup nest, the Long-tailed Tit *(Aegithalos caudatus)* for its domed home, and the tiny Goldcrest *(Regulus regulus)* for attaching its pendent cup to the underside of a twiggy conifer branch.

Left
A Long-tailed Tit *(Aegithalos caudatus)* feeds its young at its elaborate nest built of cobwebs, lichen and hair, and lined with hundreds of soft feathers.

Above
Eider Duck chicks *(Somateria mollissima)* swaddled in soft down plucked from the mother's breast in the basic structure built of seaweed and shore plants.

Right
The tidy woven nest of a Marsh Warbler *(Acrocephalus palustris)* with a parent removing a faecal sac from the nest to keep it clean.

Left
The spotted plumage of the Greenshank *(Tringa nebularia)* chicks makes an excellent camouflage on the stone-strewn moorland home.

Right
An Ovenbird's *(Seiurus aurocapillus)* nest of clay cut open to show the inner chamber with straw lining and two eggs. Here, the eggs and young are relatively safe from predators.

Below
Not coconuts attached to the palm fronds, but nests of the Village Weaver *(Ploceus cucullatus)*. The nestlings are extremely safe in these hanging homes.

Hanging nests are certainly a master construction in the bird world giving greater protection to the arboreal architects and their families. The most renowned hanging-nest builders are the various kinds of weavers, which, as their name suggests, weave grasses into wonderful pendulous nests. Village-Weaver *(Ploceus cucullatus)* nests hang like over-ripe fruits from palm trees in tropical Africa. The Baya Weaver *(Ploceus philippinus)* constructs a long entrance tube which is an added deterrent against predators such as tree snakes. The Penduline Tit *(Remiz pendulinus)* of Europe builds its hanging nest on much the same principle as that of the tropical weaverbirds.

Some birds use twigs and grasses for their nests, but add lots of mud to bind the structure together. The birds that immediately spring to mind are all the members of the swallow family. A swallow builds up its nest of mud collected from the edge of muddy streams or ponds, with plant-fibre pellets and places them like bricks in a wall. Its nest can be stuck to a wall provided it is sheltered from the rain. This is the reason why the nest is usually placed under the eaves of a building. The swifts also need to stick their nest material together in a

cavity, but they use saliva to bond it. The Ovenbirds *(Seiurus aurocapillus)* of South America make a nest that looks like an old baker's oven, on a tree branch or fence post, out of soft clay strengthened with grasses. A pair first build a cup and then add to the walls until it is roofed in. The nesting chamber is reached by a curved corridor. The nest is sufficiently strong to last two to three years before being washed away by the rains. The birds, however, usually build a new nest every year.

Probably the largest nest construction is that made by the Malleefowl *(Leipoa ocellata)* and other megapodes. It can be 10.5 metres (35 feet) in diameter and 4.5 metres (15 feet) high. The Malleefowl form breeding pairs when they are three years old. In June, at the beginning of the southern winter, they dig a huge pit in dry sandy soil, and rake into it all the vegetable litter they can find within about 45 metres (117 feet). When the rains come and soak the litter, it begins to rot and heat is given off. In August the birds begin to mix sand with the plant material in the centre of the mound, which will form an incubation chamber. In September the female begins to lay her eggs in the chamber, which has a temperature of about 33°Centigrade (92°Fahrenheit). They cover over

the chamber after each egg is laid. The female lays an egg every two to seventeen days over a period of four months. Up to thirty-three eggs are laid. To keep the chamber at a constant temperature, the pair increase or decrease the number of leaves on the mound. It is usual for the first chick to hatch at about the time the last egg is laid. It finds its own way to the surface and pushes its beak out to have its first breath of air and have a rest. Then it totters to shade and rests for about twenty-four hours before starting to look for food.

Incubating the egg

When an egg is laid most birds incubate it by sitting on it, an exception being the Malleefowl mentioned above. The incubation period of an egg is the time between the laying and hatching of a single egg. In most species, the adult has special bare 'brood patches' on the underside during the breeding season so there is no barrier between the adult and developing egg. The waterfowl, pelicans, cormorants, darters and gannets do not have brood patches but provide heat from the webs of their feet. They cover the eggs with their huge webbed feet when incubating.

The chicks of the Ostrich *(Struthio camelus)* hatch in six weeks from a nest where several females have laid their eggs. As seen here, one hen and one cock (the black and white bird) take over the brood. The chicks are well developed at birth with eyes open and a full covering of down. They are ready to walk and feed within minutes of drying their plumage.

Some birds, such as the Snowy Owl *(Nyctea scandiaca)*, begin to incubate their eggs as soon as the first egg is laid so that the chicks hatch at intervals. In the majority of birds, incubation is started when the last egg is laid. The earlier-laid eggs are not harmed by receiving only intermittent warmth and even undergo some development. However, if the chick inside the egg gets too cold later in its development, it often dies. All baby birds break out of their eggs by their own efforts. Apart from those of the Ostrich *(Struthio camelus)* and megapode families, the chick has a tooth at the tip of the upper bill which it uses to produce the first opening in the shell. It wriggles and stretches its head and legs to burst the shell open. The chick then dries off and is soon moving and ready for feeding.

The newborn chick

Just as in baby mammals, some chicks are very well-developed and others are poorly developed at birth. The well-developed chicks can move around and feed themselves within hours. These chicks are called nidifugous or precocial

nestlings and they are always born with downy feathers and with their eyes open. Ducks and waders have this type of chick and soon lead them to water where there is plenty of food for the young to find. Pheasant and Chicken *(Gallus gallus)* nestlings soon hop out of the nest on to the ground and follow the hen, who constantly calls to them. They feed alongside her, instinctively pecking at every speck. This initial trial-and-error feeding behaviour soon results in them learning which bits are edible. Gulls' chicks are well-developed at birth, but the majority are born on cliff ledges and so instinctively they stay near the nest and are fed by their parents.

The other type of nestling is the one that on hatching is naked, blind and helpless, and wholly dependent on its parents. This type of nestling is called nidicolous or altricial. The typical nidicolous nestling is a songbird baby, such as a thrush, wren, lyrebird, flycatcher and finch. Other altricial young include the pelicans, gannets, cormorants, pigeons, parrots, kingfishers and woodpeckers.

Left
Most owls begin incubation of their eggs as soon as the first egg is laid. This results in staggered hatching of the nestlings as seen in this Short-eared Owl *(Asio flammeus).* In years when food is plentiful all will probably survive; when food is scarce the first ones to hatch will have the advantage.

Below
Great Spotted Woodpecker *(Dendrocopos major)* nestlings are blind, naked and helpless at birth, and totally dependent on their parents for food.

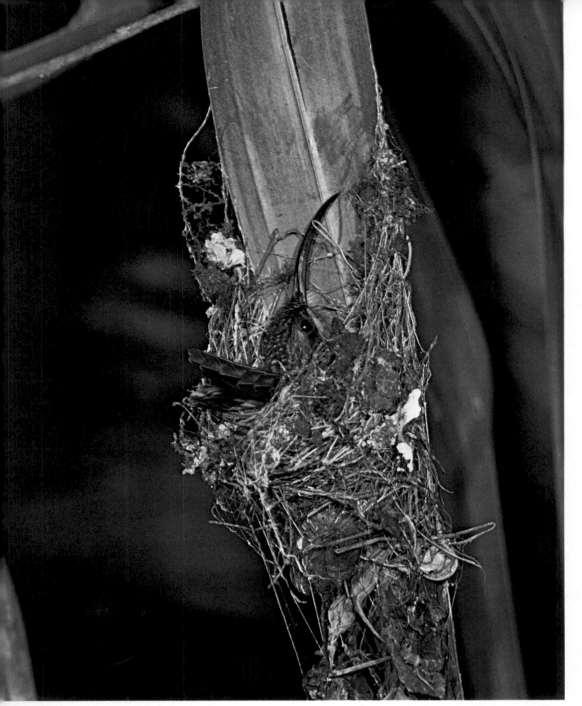

Feeding the young

The helpless nestlings are very demanding and keep their parents busy from dawn to dusk bringing them food. Although the normal diet of the adult bird may be plant material, such as seeds and fruit, the growing chicks are usually fed on grubs and insects, which are rich in protein needed to sustain their rapid development and growth. As a result, many birds have their chicks when grubs and caterpillars are plentiful. Tits, for example, coincide their babies' birth in spring with the plentiful source of leaf-eating caterpillars. A pair of Great Tits *(Parus major)* is estimated to feed its eight to twelve youngsters 7 000 to 8 000 caterpillars and other insects over the three-week period until the youngsters are fledged. Rooks *(Corvus frugilegus)* and Blackbirds *(Turdus merula)* have their chicks in early spring when the ground is soft enough to be turned over by the adult birds for worms and leaf-litter creatures. The swallows, swifts and martins feed their young on a similar diet to their own – insects, which the adults catch on the wing. They do not have their chicks until late spring and early summer when the insects are plentiful.

Some young birds take food directly from the parent's throat. A young pelican, for example, is naked and blind when born and is fed at first by the adult dribbling regurgitated food out of the end of

Above
A Rufous-breasted Hummingbird *(Selasphorus rufus)* sitting on its tiny nest. Usually hummingbirds have only one or two nestlings and feed the offspring hovering on the wing.

Right
A pigeon nestling taking its mother's 'milk', which is high in protein and boosts growth, from her crop. The nest is a simple, untidy platform of twigs, stuck together with droppings.

its beak into the chick's open mouth. After a few days the chick can see and is covered with a soft white down. It is now strong enough to stick its head into its parent's pouch to obtain food. Before the chicks are two weeks old they leave the nest and form noisy juvenile groups, but their parents still feed them for several weeks.

Pigeon young also put their beaks inside the adult's opened beak to obtain some of their food. The parent produces a secretion in its crop which looks like a cheesy mass, and is known as 'pigeon's milk'. Pigeons are unique in the bird world

in producing this milk, which is similar in composition to that of mammals. The young are fed on it about twice a day, and they store it in their crop. This boosts the young's protein intake and helps them to grow quickly. Other young birds that are fed by regurgitation include gannets, cormorants, shags and swifts.

Another method used by the young to obtain food is begging behaviour. A hungry young Herring Gull (Larus argentatus) will beg for food by pecking at the red spot on its parent's bill. This stimulates the adult to regurgitate the food on

Fluffy Little Bittern chicks (Ixobrychus minutus) and attentive parent. One chick is pecking at the parent's beak, attempting to get regurgitated food.

Below
The brightly coloured gapes of many nestlings instinctively attract a parent to push in food. Here Dunnock *(Prunella modularis)* chicks beg for food.

Far right
Alert Martial Eagles *(Polemaetus bellicosus)* with their single chick. The same nest is used year after year with just new fresh green leaves added from time to time to line the nest.

to the ground in front of the chick. Birds of prey such as hawks, eagles and owls, tear up the prey when the young are small. The babies feed on these tiny morsels but soon are able to manage larger pieces and can deal with a carcase by themselves in two or three weeks. The shrikes also dismember prey for their nestlings. They are often called butcherbirds due to their habit of impaling prey such as grasshoppers and lizards on the thorns of bushes.

Most song-birds, and many other species, simply bring food such as insects or caterpillars in the bill and push it more or less whole into the wide-open beaks of the nestlings. The nestlings cry out to attract the parent to them and the inside colouring of the bill (the gape) stimulates the parent to feed them. The colour of the gape varies with each species, some having bright spots or other markings against a white, red or black background.

The time it takes from hatching to flying (the fledging period) varies from species to species. Megapodes can practically fly when they struggle out of their huge nest mound. Ptarmigan *(Lagopus mutus)* chicks fly after about ten days and other game birds such as pheasants and quails take two weeks. All these birds continue to grow after they have learnt to fly. Most small song-birds can fly in under two weeks, while the majority of the passerines, including pigeons, hummingbirds and bee-eaters, take three weeks. Cormorants, storks, some large owls and hornbills cannot fly until they are nearly eight weeks old and pelicans may take a week longer. There are only a few birds that have really long fledging periods. Swifts are not able to fly until nearly ten weeks old in the years when insects are not very numerous. The Osprey *(Pandion haliaetus)* and crane babies also take ten weeks to develop sufficiently to take to the air. Most eagles and Barn Owls *(Tyto alba)* do not fly under eleven weeks and the Griffon Vulture *(Gyps fulvus)* young take another week. The albatrosses have exceptionally long fledging periods, the smaller ones taking twenty to twenty-one weeks while the Royal Albatross takes thirty-six weeks, or occasionally longer.

Intensive observation by ornithologists has revealed that in various species, including grebes and some song-birds, the parents may divide the brood between them as soon as the young leave the nest.

One adult accepts responsibility for feeding some of the young, but will neglect the remaining ones, these being the responsibility of the other parent. They even behave aggressively towards the chicks not in their batch.

Even when the babies have learnt to fly and left the nest, some still spend a lot of time with their parents, begging for food, fluttering and calling. It is known that swans and geese and their growing cygnets stay as a family throughout the first winter of the young. The babblers are exceptional in that the young may stay and assist their parents with the next nesting. For most young, however, the final break with their parents occurs during the autumn moult, the birds now being adult and usually finding partners for breeding their own young by the following spring.

Unusual babies

The Emperor Penguin *(Aptenodytes forsteri)* male, the largest of the penguins, incubates the single egg on his feet with warmth provided by the skin of the lower abdomen. The female, who goes away during the incubation period to feed, returns just in time for hatching.

In the world of birds, one of the most interesting breeding habits is that of the large Emperor Penguins *(Aptenodytes forsteri)* of Antarctica. No nest is built for the egg, one important reason being that there is only ice and snow available to the parents as building materials. Instead the female lays one egg and immediately passes it over to her mate who collects it on his large webbed feet. She then travels 80–160 kilometres (50–100 miles) to the sea to feed, while he settles down and covers the egg with the fold of his feathered lower belly. There the egg is kept snug and warm and hatches about sixty-four days later. The baby sits on the adult's feet, poking its head out to look at the world. The female returns within a day or so, and the male goes off to feed, having lost about 30 per cent of his body weight during his prolonged fast. The chick obtains food regurgitated from the female's crop. They grow quite quickly and begin to leave the warmth and safety of their parents' feet. They are covered with long, dark brown down. They have a long childhood spending much time huddled together with other youngsters in creches, while the parents go fishing for food. The Emperor Penguins establish their breeding colony where the pack ice breaks up early so the adults soon do not have far to travel for food. The chicks fledge in December or January, when there is an abundance of food in Antarctic waters.

Some birds, the most well-known example being the cuckoos, avoid sitting on their own eggs by laying them in another bird's nest. The female European Cuckoo *(Cuculus canorus)* returns from wintering in South Africa or south-west Asia and searches for the nest of a Dunnock *(Prunella modularis),* Redstart *(Phoenicurus phoenicurus),* or some other species, in which to lay her eggs. The female lays a single egg in the nest while the host is away from her home. There are probably some of her eggs already in the nest and the Cuckoo usually takes one of the eggs away so that on the return of the potential host, there are still the same number of eggs in the nest. Although the Cuckoo's egg is larger and more sturdy than the host's eggs, it closely matches them in colour.

The female host rarely notices the change in her nest and happily incubates the Cuckoo's egg with her own eggs. During the first few hours after hatching, although it is blind and naked, the baby Cuckoo instinctively hoists the other eggs or baby chicks over the edge of the nest, using its back and wings. At last it is the only survivor and as a result gets all the attention and food from the ever-busy foster parents. By the time it is half-grown it is quite large and much bigger than its foster parents who, however, still accept it as their own offspring. At three-weeks old the cuckoo has outgrown its foster parents' nest,

Above
A Dunnock *(Prunella modularis),* the deceived foster parent, feeds an almost fledged Cuckoo *(Cuculus canorus),* clinging to its giant foster child's head in order to put food into the ever-hungry bird's beak.

Left
Adelie Penguin *(Pygoscelis adeliae)* 'auntie' tending young Adelies in their creche, while other parents go fishing for food.

Right
A Collie bitch makes an unusual foster mother for a young badger that has lost its parents.

Below
The bright golden colouring of the young Spectacled Langur enables the mother to locate it quickly.

Far right
Baby Wild Boar *(Sus scrofa)* snuggling together. Some people think the stripes are for camouflage while others believe they are an identification signal for the mother.

but it is fledged and can find food for itself. Very soon afterwards it flies south to Africa or south-west Asia for the winter with no help from any adult cuckoos. These birds have departed already to seek the sun and food.

The cowbirds of North America and honeyguides of Africa are other birds that parasitize other birds' nests with their eggs and offspring. The female cowbird keeps a close watch on the progress of nest-building in her host which is often a meadowlark, or a warbler, vireo or sparrow. She knows just when to lay, visiting the nest for only a few minutes to lay her egg and quickly departing. Not all species will accept the cowbird parasitism. It is known that the Catbird *(Dumetella cardinensis)* throws out foreign eggs and the little Yellow Warbler *(Motacilla flava)* sometimes builds a new nest on top of the one with the foreign egg.

Foster parents are sometimes found by man for his domesticated animals that have been deserted at birth by the mother. Goats have suckled lambs and a ewe has mothered an orphan piglet. Sometimes a

mother animal is deprived of her own young and her normal rhythm of maternal behaviour is upset. As a result she may take to mothering almost any small animal she comes into contact with, even if the species is totally different. Baboons have been known to adopt kittens, as have bitches and even broody hens. It has even been known for a mother cat to adopt baby mice or rabbits, which are usually her prey.

Mammalian babies are sometimes completely different in coloration to their parents. Perhaps the strangest colouring is found in the Spectacled Langur baby. It is born with a bright golden covering of hair, while its parents are mainly black apart from startling white 'spectacles' around their eyes. This special colouring evokes parental behaviour in the adults. A langur family is a very caring family. As a langur mother holds her newborn baby, cleaning and inspecting its tiny body, the other females of the group gather around eager to touch the baby. Within a few hours the mother allows other females to hold it, but she keeps a close watch on her tiny orange bundle, the colour again

helping her to keep visual contact. At the slightest alarm she will dash to her baby and scoop it up, the other females recognizing the mother's right. Once the growing infant's coat changes colour, at about five to six months, the attitude of the females changes. They no longer want to hold it and give it cuddles. The mother, however, still remains protective and although the youngster spends much time learning from playing with other young langurs, its mother is always ready to come to its rescue if needed.

Certain young animals, such as young terns, plovers, oyster-catchers and deer fawns, are coloured to match their surroundings. They would probably not survive if they were the colour of their parents, since, if spotted by a predator, they would be unable to escape. It is usually thought that young Wild Boar are spotted and striped for the same reason. This is probably not the case, however, as observations made on the behaviour of young Wild Pigs suggest a more acceptable reason. When danger threatens, the youngsters do not lie down and let their colours blend in with the

Right
The spotted and striped coat of this baby
Malayan Tapir *(Tapirus indicus)* probably
serves as camouflage on the sun- or
moon-dappled floor of its jungle home.

Left
Unlike most ant-lion larvae, the 45-millimetre (1·8-inch) long Giant Ant-lion *(Palpares inclemens)* of South Africa does not build a pit but hides in soft sand with only its large, pincer jaws protruding. Here it has grasped a 30-millimetre (1·2-inch) long grasshopper which passed too close.

Below
The beast becomes a beauty; the ant-lion larva after pupation emerges as a delicately winged flying adult.

bracken and ground vegetation. They immediately bolt to their mother rather than hide. In addition, the mother does not leave them as, for example, a mother deer leaves her fawn. A Wild Boar sow will ferociously defend her young. So it seems the spots and stripes are a social signal (as in the langurs), bringing out the appropriate responses from the mother and other adults.

The spotted and striped coat of a young tapir does seem to serve as camouflage. In the Malayan Tapir *(Tapirus indicus)* the baby is dark brown with tawny spots and streaks, and blends into the sun- or moon-dappled forest floor of the jungle home. The parent has a striking coat of contrasting areas of black and white. In the jungle the adult is active during the night and the white midsection of the adult breaks the animal into two. To a hunter, such as a Tiger, the broken body does not suggest the form of a complete animal since the head, shoulders and front legs, and the rump and hind legs are obscured. So the contrasting coats of adult and baby serve to hide them from predators.

The ant lion may be compared to the beast in the well-loved fairy tale, 'Beauty and the Beast'. The youngster is a rather vicious predator trapping ants in sand pits, and changes into a beautiful dragonfly-like adult, which feeds on fruit and small flies. The female lays its eggs in sand. Within a day of hatching the larva has dug a pit about 50 millimetres (2 inches) deep and 75 millimetres (3 inches) in diameter. This pit is one of the most spectacular traps in the animal kingdom, despite its small size. Buried at the bottom of its pit, with only its head and strong biting jaws exposed, the larva waits for grains of sand, disturbed by a passing ant or spider, to roll down the sides of its pit. As the sand hits the larva it triggers off the trapping action. The larva jerks its head forwards and upwards, catapulting a stream of sand over the pit's brim.

Right
An African Mouthbrooder *(Haplochromis burtoni)* female spits out a mouthful of babies she has just retrieved from the edge of her territory.

Far right
Busy worker bees feeding the grub-like larvae, each one requiring over 1000 portions of pollen a day.

This barrage showers the intended victim and, together with the steep sides of the pit, causes the victim to slide down into the pit. The larva immediately seizes it in its jaws and when it has a good grip on the prey, it injects paralysing fluid into the prey's body. Once sedated, the larva injects digestive juices in much the same way and slowly, as the tissues dissolve, the ant lion sucks them up. The ant lion lives like this for one to three years, moulting about three times and eventually spends a period pupating inside a silken cocoon before emerging as a beautiful delicately winged adult.

A most unusual way of caring for the young takes place inside a beehive. Although thousands of bees live and work inside the colony, only one female lays the eggs. This is the large queen bee, which after mating with a male bee (a drone) in the air spends the rest of her life laying eggs. She can lay up to 3000 a day. She is so busy that she has no time to care for her offspring and this is left to the thousands of worker bees, which are sterile females.

Each egg is laid inside its own hexagonal wax cell constructed by the workers. It hatches into a grub-like larva and is cared for by the workers. It feeds on pollen, sheds its skin several times, and after about six days it spins a cocoon and pupates. Twelve days later, when it hatches from its pupal case, it is a perfectly formed bee, the majority being workers, and a few males. Queen bees are produced by special feeding techniques, and only when a colony is coming to the end in autumn.

For about the first two weeks, a young bee's principal occupation is that of a nurse. It brings honey and pollen from the storage cells to feed the queen, the males or drones and the larvae. This is a very demanding job as a single larva eats over 1000 portions of pollen a day. As the bee gets older it is able to produce wax from glands on the underside of its body and so it passes on to a new profession – that of building combs. This is middle-age in the life of a bee and other duties at this time include taking care of the hive, cleaning and standing guard at its entrance, stinging any intruder, such as a bee from another colony or a visiting mouse.

We have mentioned that the amphibians, such as frogs, newts and toads, do not usually look after their young. A few amphibians do, however, and a most unusual and interesting method of caring for the young eggs and tadpoles is found in the South American arrow-poison frogs. After the eggs have been laid and fertilized, they become attached to the male's back, although how

this is done remains to be discovered. Here they hatch into small tadpoles and they cling there, getting no moisture except rainwater. Up to twenty tadpoles have been found on one male's back, and as they grow larger, the male seeks larger and larger holes in which to rest. Eventually he takes them down to the water and they swim away to lead an independent life.

The story of Peter Pan, the young boy who never grew up, is well known. In the animal world there is a true Peter Pan, the axolotyl, a strange-looking amphibian which lives in lakes near Mexico City in Central America. It is a newt-like creature, usually black or brown although albino (white forms) are quite common. It breathes through three pairs of feathery gills situated on the sides of the head. It never leaves the water and does not develop into an adult newt which can come out on to land, but is able to breed in its larval state. Scientists have discovered that an axolotyl will change into a salamander if given thyroxine extract from the thyroid gland, a hormone that controls the metabolism of the body. It contains iodine in its composition and this is lacking in the water where the axolotyl lives so that it does not metamorphose.

Another interesting freshwater animal is the Bitterling *(Rhodeus sericeus)*, a small European fish which forms breeding pairs and then searches for a freshwater mussel. The female extends a short egg-laying tube (ovipositor) and deposits her eggs inside the mussel's shells. The male sheds his sperm inside and the eggs are left to develop in the safety of the mussel. When the small Bitterling fry hatch they stay inside the mussel for about a month, feeding on minute food particles drawn in by the mussel.

Above
A Viviparous Lizard *(Lacerta vivipara)* with its new babies. A Eurasian species, it usually inhabits cool places such as mountain slopes. After mating in early spring the young develop inside the mother's body and are born live in the warm summer, the young babies soon struggling free from their transparent birth sacs.

Left
A female Bitterling *(Rhodeus sericeus)* with her long egg-laying ovipositor positioned between the open shells of a pond mussel. The male will shed his milt immediately she has deposited her eggs.

Male seahorse with the brood pouch on his belly, in which the female lays her eggs, clearly visible. To expel the baby seahorses when they have hatched, the male contracts and relaxes his body.

The strange-looking seahorses have probably the most unusual breeding habits of all fishes. As a pair of seahorses begin to court one another, the male swims in front of his mate and appears to bow to her. In fact he is pumping water out of the pouch on his belly. The female inserts her long egg-laying tube through the pouch's large opening and lays up to 200 eggs, the male shedding his sperm at the same time to fertilize them. By the time laying is finished the opening to the pouch has become a minute pore and it stays like this until the baby seahorses are ready to be born, in four to five weeks. When the young hatch, the pouch opening enlarges and the male bends and straightens his body in jerks shooting tiny 12-millimetre (0·5-inch) long miniature seahorse babies into the water. It is an extremely exhausting process for the male. These tiny babies immediately swim to the surface of the water to fill their swimbladders with air, and then start feeding on tiny crustaceans, such as newly hatched brine shrimps.

Index

Page numbers in italic refer to illustrations.

Acknowledgements

ARDEA: I. R. Beames 17B, 82, Tony Beamish 29, Hans Beste 37, R.M. Bloomfield 83, Donald T. Burgess 69A, Elizabeth S. Burgess 13, John Clegg 65B, Werner Curth 43, M.D. England 80A, Jean-Paul Ferrero 15, Kenneth W. Fink 12, 66–67, Paul Germain 54, John Gooders 78, Su Gooders 24–25, M.E.J. Gore 76B, Don Hadden 36, Peter Laub 75, Eric Lindgren 69B, Pat Morris 11A, C.K. Mylne 79A, S. Roberts 22, Peter Steyn 32A, Ron Taylor 56B, John Wightman 48A; BIOFOTOS: 10, 55, 59, 65A; CAMERA PRESS: 16; BRUCE COLEMAN LTD: Helmot Albrecht 47, Jen and Des Bartlett 38B, 58A, 66A, S. C. Bisserot 32, Jeffrey Boswall 77, Jane Burton 17A, 53, 62, 64, 68, 90, Gerald Cubitt 20, Francisco Erize 40–41, Jeff Foott 58B, Dennis Green 80B, Leonard Lee Rue III 38A, 51, Norman R. Lightfoot 57, Lee Lyon 28, John Markham 35, N. Myers 49, Oxford Scientific Films 60A, Allan Power 94, Masood Quarishy 42, Hans Reinhard 19, 23, 27, 31, 50; RICHARD COOKE: Title page; JAMES CROSS: 26; JOHN DOIDGE: 86B; ERIC HOSKING: 76A; JACANA: Suirot 84; KEYSTONE PRESS AGENCY: 56A; FRANK W. LANE: Franz Hartmann 46, W. C. Wright 74R, R. S. Virdee 48B; THOR LARSEN: 30; FRANCOIS MERLET: 70; MICRO COLOUR LTD: 86A; NATURAL HISTORY PHOTOGRAPHIC AGENCY: Joe B. Blossom 93, Anthony Bannister 88A, 89, Stephen Dalton 60B, 65C, 74L, 85A, 91, Peter Johnson 85B; NATURFOTO (PAUL STAROSTA/ATLAS): 14; OXFORD SCIENTIFIC FILMS: 8–9, 11B; KLAUS PAYSAN: 44A, 44B, 45, 63, 88B; LAURENCE E. PERKINS: 92; TONY STONE ASSOCIATES: 7, 18, 21, 39, 61, 71, 81, 87; Z.E.F.A.: W. Kratz 33, Hans Reinhard 6, F. Rust endpapers, Shostal 34, W. Tilgner 79B.